(VEG)ETABLES	FISH SEAFOODS	MEATS	POULTRY		(D)ESSERTS, (BR)EADS, ROLLS
...ots, ...ry	Sole, Crab				...es, Cookies, ...et rolls
...atoes, ...ons	Shrimp creole	Beef, Pork, Veal, Lamb			
...ach, ...s	Shellfish	All kinds	All kinds & stuffings	Cream sauces	
...aragus, ...hrooms	Shellfish			Tartar sauce, Wine vinegar	
...bage, ...toes, ...iflower		Casseroles, German dishes		Applesauce	Cookies, Bread, Apple pie, Cakes
...toes, ...atoes, ...kinds	Shellfish, Broiled fish	All kinds	All kinds	Tartar sauce, Butter sauces, Wine vinegar	
...bage, ...liflower, ...atoes	Halibut, Salmon	Lamb, Ham	Creamed chicken	Tartar sauce, Butter sauces, Wine vinegar	Rye bread
...ots, ...ach, ...sh	Baked or Broiled fish	All kinds	Chicken, Duck, Goose	Gravies, Fish sauces	Biscuits, Muffins
...en beans, ...y peas	Baked or Broiled fish	Lamb, Veal		Mint sauces, Wine vinegar	Mint syrups, Sherbets, etc.
...ons, Peas, ...ed beans	Shellfish	All kinds	Game, Hare, Venison	Cream sauce, Tomato sauce	Meat-pie crusts, Breads
...kinds	All kinds	All kinds	Stuffing	Tartar sauce, Butter sauces	Breads, Rolls
...atoes, ...shrooms	Salmon, Haddock, Cod	All kinds	Stuffings, Wild game	Gravies	Bread, Rolls, Biscuits
...plant, ...a beans	Baked or Broiled fish	Meat loaf, Roasts	Stuffings, Turkey, Game	Brown sauce	Muffins, Breads
...en beans, ...erkraut	Salt-water fish	All kinds	Chicken, Duck, Turkey	Fish sauces, Cream sauce	Meat-pie crusts
...aragus	All fish	Steaks	Chicken, Duck, Turkey	Cream sauce, Hollandaise	
...ns, Onions, ...atoes	All kinds	Roasts, Meat loaf, Ham	Stuffings, Turkey	All tomato sauces	Breads, Rolls

Everyday Cooking with Herbs

Everyday Cooking with Herbs

Mary A. Collin

WITH THE FOOD EDITORS OF *Farm Journal*

SPECIAL SECTION: How to Grow Your Own

Illustrations by Al J. Reagan
Farm Journal Art Staff

DOUBLEDAY & COMPANY, INC.
Garden City, New York

ISBN: 0-385-07641-x
Library of Congress Catalog Card Number 73–81123
Copyright © 1952, 1974 by Farm Journal, Inc.
All Rights Reserved
Printed in the United States of America

To my family—Barbara, Carleton, Margaret and Robert, who helped with the herb business, and who ate my experimental dishes with tolerance and encouragement.

Contents

PART II

Everyday Cooking with Herbs

How I Got into the Herb Business

Growing herbs can be a fascinating hobby, a small home industry, or, if you have the know-how, the land and the capital, a lucrative business. It's even possible to progress from one to the other. How could I know that the Scotch Ridge Herb Farm was in my future the day I visited the Bishop's Garden at Washington National Cathedral and bought six little plants— as an experiment?

That was 30 years ago, but I still remember the Bishop's Garden. The plot was large, the many beds set apart and bordered with boxwood. In one area we discovered the beauty and fragrance of the lavenders: English, with its gray narrow leaves and purple flowers; French, with narrower, more silvery leaves, not so high a plant, the flowers a deeper purple; and spike, with broader, spatulate leaves and tall flower stalks. We were intrigued by the number of herb varieties, the contrasts of leaf colors and textures, flower sizes, colors and shapes, and the tantalizing aromas these plants produced.

When we got back to our Chevy Chase home, I planted my new herbs under the quince tree in the backyard—and immediately found our neighbors curious and enthusiastic about the little plants. What could I tell them? At that time, little more than the names: English lavender, sweet basil, winter savory, sweet marjoram, rosemary, and French tarragon.

Our little herb patch in Washington grew as our interest grew; we added not only more cooking herbs, but fragrant and medicinal herbs as well. My own research into the uses of the various herbs absorbed all the time I could spare from family demands.

During World War II we moved to Michigan, almost next door to a Michigan herb expert. We soon became friends. She had many herbs we didn't have, but we had brought some

herbs from the East she didn't have. So, we began the common
and rewarding habit of trading seeds, cuttings and layerings.

A year or two later we moved from Lansing to Kalamazoo,
and found a house with acreage we thought well suited to growing herbs. That first year we planted 7 rows, perhaps 6 feet
long, or altogether about 42 plants: basil, chives, sage, marjoram, savory, French tarragon and English thyme. We harvested them before frost, dried and stored them. Moving always pinches the pocketbook, so when Christmas drew near, I
hit upon the idea of making little herb chests for our friends
and relatives. We collected empty cigar boxes from tobacco
stores, which I painted in gay colors, composing a brief poem
about herbs to paste on the inside of the lids:

> We've heard it said, it's not *what* you give,
> But the loving thought that counts;
> So you'll find in this little Christmas box
> Six jars, each containing an ounce
> Of some herbs we've grown in our garden,
> And a jar of herb jelly too;
> We hope you'll use and enjoy them,
> For they're bringing our love to you.

It wasn't difficult to persuade our pharmacist to sell me several dozen 1-ounce jars with screw tops, and I made my own
labels. I packed each box with 6 jars of herbs and a jar of herb
jelly; my gifts cost almost nothing, and they were really attractive.

At that time I was office manager for a hospital building
campaign. The girls with whom I worked admired the herb
chests and asked me to fill more for their own use. I put together as many as I could, saving out a few to take to a local
department store which featured a gourmet shop. The buyer
was interested and encouraging: If I'd package them in attractive containers with colorful labels and put them together in
suitable gift boxes, she'd purchase a few dozen as a start.

This opened up a whole new world! What kind of boxes,
what size, and how many? Should I count on only a single-
outlet operation or try to sell herbs in other cities? What kind of

labels? What kind of bottles and jars . . . where does one find them?

But first, the herbs—if we were going to try a cottage industry, we'd have to lay out an area for growing herbs in quantity; and how many varieties should we grow? Through the rest of that winter we combed through catalogs and discovered that almost every seed company carries a few kinds of herb seeds. Plants that were too slow growing from seed would have to be ordered. That presented another problem. Some of the nurseries and greenhouses in the area carried a few plants, so when spring came we'd have to make layerings and cuttings of our own plants like mad.

We also named our venture: Scotch Ridge Herb Farm. Our land was on a ridge; a century or more ago, relatives settled at a small place in Ohio which they called Scotch Ridge, and of course, they were all Scotsmen. Besides, I could use a Scotch plaid for my labels and a theme.

I tracked down a paper-box maker in the Yellow Pages and obtained prices for boxes of three different sizes, to be made by the hundred or the thousand—they were too expensive in smaller quantities. I also found several bottle manufacturers located in Chicago, called and asked for prices on different sizes of glass bottles and jars. I found a local printer who specialized in labels and got prices for these. Designing the label was as easy as copying a simple Scotch plaid. For the person launching a cottage industry, an attractive label is definitely one of the factors which helps sell your product. It's worth some time and thought, even some professional help, to develop a design that's simple and appropriate, that people will remember. These days, labels can be printed in volume on pressure-sensitive paper.

Through the winter we collected all the seeds we would need for the quick-growing herbs: basil, burnet, dill, sage, parsley, savory and thyme. We managed to find lemon balm plants; we had our own chive plants to multiply by digging up the clumps and dividing the bulblets; it was easy to buy garlic bulbs and divide them. We layered our own sweet marjoram, mints, orégano, rosemary and tarragon. That first "commercial" year we had all the plants I could manage to process for dried herbs.

But drying such quantities presented a problem. Drying by the natural process of dehydration takes too long, the herbs lose their color, and much of the aromatic oil evaporates. A commercial dryer that would accommodate several bushels of herbs must somehow be constructed.

To house the dryer and to get all the work done, we had to build an "herb house"—where we could bring the herbs in from the garden to wash them, plus an area for processing after drying, where the bottling and labeling could be done, and the packing. We planned a 3-room building back of our garage, to house a drying room, a processing room and a sales/display room—already, we'd had many visitors to our little herb plot, not only local people but others from outlying towns and cities.

When we built the herb house, we put a 16-foot-long counter underneath a bank of windows facing south, where we could winter our tender perennials—such as rosemary and the scented geraniums we had by then begun to collect—and where we also could start flats the following spring. We added storage cabinets under the counters for the gallon jars of the herb wine vinegars, Herb Mustard and Herb French Dressing which need to be aged. In the processing room we installed a large double-well sink for washing the herbs, and space to store large pans, trays, screens and other equipment.

But we still didn't know how to build a good dryer: a real problem. We wrote to several commercial growers, but apparently drying herbs commercially is a closely guarded secret. By trial and error, we constructed our own. We made a plywood cabinet about 6 feet high by 3 feet square, fitting it with sliding shelves of window screening in thin wooden frames. Providing the proper heat was the greatest problem. By installing a space heater, a blower, and a large pipe leading into the floor of the dryer, we were finally able to dry from 4 to 6 bushels of herbs a day efficiently. We could regulate the temperature so that the leaves dried at the proper rate of speed, thus retaining their color and aroma.

After drying, the leaves are stripped from their stems and rubbed over a wire screen made of ¼-inch mesh. Then they are ready for bottling and labeling.

The first year we packed small Scotch plaid boxes which held either 6 1-ounce jars of herbs, 3 3-ounce bottles of herb wine vinegars, or 2 jars of herbs and 2 bottles of the vinegars. The herb wine vinegars were easy to make (you'll find the recipes in this book). The department store buyer who had promised to purchase some of my wares was pleased with the appearance of Scotch Ridge packages and took more than half of all I had that season. When we grew larger, we added a greater variety of box sizes and combinations of products.

Meantime, evenings and in all my so-called spare time, I was reading all the herb books I could find—books about their history, their propagation and culture, their uses in medicine and industry. Word got around that I was an "herb expert." Invitations to speak about herbs began to come in from local garden clubs and women's clubs.

It isn't easy to describe the courage it took for a shy, timid woman to stand up in front of a group of strangers and talk. It had always been difficult for me even to recite in school. But if the herb project were to continue and succeed, I'd have to learn to talk about it. The first herb lecture was agony; but like jumping into cold water, once you make the plunge it isn't so bad.

By word-of-mouth (Mrs. A., who'd been in the audience at the first talk, wrote to Mrs. B., in Chicago or Detroit, saying they'd found a new speaker), I began to receive invitations to speak in other cities, offering me a specific lecture fee plus travel expenses. Eventually I was speaking to groups of five hundred or more.

As the speaking dates became more frequent, I devised my own way of establishing outlets for my herb products: Wherever I traveled, I took along a small case of my herbs and looked up the best gourmet shop in the town. I'd tell the buyer I was speaking at such-and-such a club that afternoon, and that the women would want to know where they could buy the products. If I could give the audience the name of a local dealer, and if he would take the case of herbs I'd brought with me on consignment, I felt sure he'd sell out in a day or two. That's exactly what happened everywhere I went—through 28 states. Of course this didn't transpire all at once . . . but at the end of 10 years we had over 200 retailers in these states, who ordered and reordered steadily.

At the beginning of our third commercial year, we decided to build a formal herb garden, a "showplace" for visitors. We laid out a replica in miniature of the herb garden at Blenheim Palace, 40 feet square, with a center path of flagstones. Garden clubs made tours of the place, my son and daughter acting as guides. From June to October, there was hardly a day when we didn't have visitors wandering around the garden.

We also expanded the commercial growing area to meet the demand for Scotch Ridge products. We planted 100-foot rows of herbs down the length of the back acreage. These rows included 4 thymes—English, golden, silver and lemon—orégano, rosemary, sage, winter savory, sweet basil, sweet marjoram, burnet, chives, the mints—apple, orange, lemon, pineapple, spearmint, as well as curly and woolly mint—anise, lemon balm, caraway, chervil, garlic, horehound, English lavender, parsley, pennyroyal, santolina, southernwood, French tarragon, rue and wormwood. Under a giant apple tree, where they would live in partial shade, we planted our garden collection of scented geraniums; we carpeted the ground under a big wild cherry tree with ajuga; and in another shady spot beneath an apple tree we had a large area of sweet woodruff. Thirty of these were culinary herbs which we grew for processing. The rest we sold as plants to gardeners who wanted their old-fashioned herb gardens to include more than the culinary herbs.

By now planting, weeding, harvesting, washing, drying, processing, packaging, labeling, and shipping took the greater part of all my days. We harvested several times a year, for the tender young tops of the herbs are best. They have more aroma, are not woody, and dry more quickly. Also, the plants grow more compact and bushy if the top growth is clipped frequently.

Our Scotch Ridge line finally included 10 varieties of dried herbs, 7 herb wine vinegars, 8 herb jellies, 4 herb blends, and the two most popular items of all, our Herb Mustard and Herb French Dressing. These last two were unique. I worked on the formulas for several years, experimenting until I found the perfect combination of herbs for each product. We shipped each of them by the case to most of our dealers. The Herb Mustard and Herb French Dressing accounted for at least 50 per cent of the business. Even now, after all these years, I still receive cards, letters and telephone calls asking for these two herb mixtures. The recipes for both are included in this book—I give them to you, and you'll find them outstanding.

MARY COLLIN

PART I

Herbs for Variety in Everyday Meals

For centuries both men and women have sought new ways to make food more palatable and meals more varied and interesting. We have a plentiful supply of food, and we can prepare and serve almost anything out-of-season, thanks to modern-day technology. But the solution to day-by-day meal variety is basically seasoning. Not just salt and pepper, but *herbs*.

In our servantless society, sooner or later almost everyone takes a turn in the kitchen, or at the barbecue grill. Families are more adventurous than they used to be about visiting foreign-fare restaurants. At dinner parties and backyard picnics, both men and women talk about food, sharing their cooking secrets with enthusiasm: fresh chopped basil on tomatoes . . . how a tiny pinch of dill improves shrimp . . . Herb Salt for hamburgers . . . Tarragon Wine Vinegar in the salad dressing . . . .

Many women complain that "herb recipes are too complicated" or that "it takes too long to make sauces and concoct fancy seasoning mixtures." This is a legitimate complaint. There *has* been too much "secret recipe" mystique about herbs.

In reality, herb cookery can be quite simple. This book fills the need for a collection of taste-teasing and eye-catching herb recipes that are quick and easy. If you do your own housework, run the family errands, and try to participate in civic and social activities, then this book is for you.

There are no hard and fast rules in the art of cooking with herbs, but there are a few hints to assist you in becoming skillful in their use. It's important to remember that the addition of an herb does not change the chemistry of the food. It merely enhances the flavor, and makes even the plainest foods more enticing.

Foods cooked with herbs are not "too highly seasoned" for everyday eating. Spices sometimes give food a highly seasoned, peppery taste, but herbs don't smother the natural taste of the food. And, many culinary herbs are extremely rich in vitamins and minerals. Of course, you use very small amounts.

Be sure your herbs are fresh—not necessarily fresh from the garden, but that the bottle of dried herbs on your shelf isn't old. You can't expect the same result from herbs which have stood for so long they've lost their aroma. Write the date on the bottle when you buy herbs, and replace them after 12 to 18 months.

You may use either fresh green herbs or dried herbs in cooking—but you must change the proportions. Dried herbs are naturally more concentrated. As a general rule, in a recipe making 4 servings, use ¼ teaspoon dried herbs, or 1 full teaspoon of the fresh green herb.

Actually, the amount of herb you use in any dish may vary from general rules or printed recipes; you should be governed by what tastes best to you and your family. When you're experimenting, remember that too little is better than too much. It's good practice to start with a pinch and add to taste. What's a pinch? Officially, a pinch is ⅟₁₆ teaspoon or about what you can hold between thumb and finger.

Don't season more than one dish in a meal with the same herb, and don't feel that every item on your menu must be "herbed." Your family and guests can tire of herbs quickly if you add them to everything you serve. Also, don't worry too much about the "proper" herb. If a recipe calls for thyme and you don't have it, experiment with a light touch of another herb. It will add a new flavor to a variety of foods, from appetizers to main dishes. For the best substitution, consult the alphabetical list found in The Most Common and Useful Culinary Herbs section, which describes the flavor and cooking uses of each herb.

The Most Common and Useful Culinary Herbs

Most supermarkets now carry a wide selection of dried herbs—you should have no trouble finding any of these in the following list. The whole herb leaves are a better choice than ground or powdered herbs; they hold their flavor longer in storage and you can always crumble or pulverize the leaves if necessary. Dried herbs should be tightly capped and stored away from heat—don't stack them on the back of the range!

The little herb racks are attractive, but if placed in the sunlight, the herbs will lose their color and flavor. The best way to keep herbs fresh and flavorful is to store them in a cool, dark place such as inside a cupboard. And don't buy the cheapest brands in tin containers; you get what you pay for, and the more expensive brand often is the best in the long run. If you can't smell the aroma when the jar is opened, or if the herbs have turned pale and grayish, they've lost their potency and should be discarded.

If you'd rather grow and dry your own herbs, you'll find propagation information and illustrations of the most commonly grown herb plants in Part II—How to Grow Your Own Herbs. Most of the following herbs will thrive in American gardens—in poor soil, with relatively little care. Several adapt themselves to indoor pot gardening.

ANGELICA: Aromatic and sweet, much like a combination of vanilla and rhubarb. The stems and leaf stalks are often eaten as celery. The candied stalks are used in cookies, cakes and candies. Both leaves and stems are excellent in herb teas (see Herb Teas and Other Beverages).

ANISE: The leaves of this herb give a mild licoricelike taste to fruit salads, applesauce, baked apples, cookies, cakes, and add a new flavor to any mild fish—sole, salmon, etc. The seeds are delicious with fruits; try heating peaches, apricots or cherries with ¼ teaspoonful of aniseeds. The seeds make a delightful tea, either mixed with orange pekoe or steeped alone. (See also Herb Teas and Other Beverages.)

BALM, LEMON: With its fresh lemon taste this herb is splendid chopped in salads, mixed with spinach, Swiss chard or any greens, and with peas. Fine for flavoring summer drinks and iced tea.

BASIL, SWEET: The clove-pepperish taste is a great addition to salads, stews, in all tomato and egg dishes, vegetable juice cocktails, on roasts, in spaghetti, or finely chopped in cottage cheese.

BAY LEAF: This herb has a taste between sage and rosemary, but milder. It's the leaf of mountain laurel grown in Greece, Spain and Portugal, and parts of Asia. Our native mountain laurel doesn't have the true taste. Use on roasts, stews, meat pies, meat loaf, poultry (both for seasoning and in stuffing) and vegetable soups.

BORAGE: The celery-cucumber flavor of the young leaves is good in vegetable salads, cooked with greens of any kind, with cabbage and coleslaw, or crushed and mixed with fruit juice for a cooling summer drink.

BURNET: The leaves of this attractive little plant are sharply cucumber in flavor. Excellent addition to all tossed salads, potato salad, and makes a delicate herb vinegar. Unusually tasty in cream of asparagus soup.

CAMOMILE, ROMAN: The lacy threadlike leaves make a delicious tea with an apple flavor. Both the leaves and tiny daisy flowers are an attractive garnish for fruit salads and in fruit punch.

CAPERS: These tiny little green flower buds of a European shrub are pickled in brine and give a distinguished flavor to seafood and chicken salad, sprinkled on fish before broiling or added to jellied vegetable salads.

CARAWAY: It's difficult to describe the flavor, but we associate it closely with the taste of rye bread. The leaves enhance any salad or soup; seeds used in rye bread, with sauerkraut, cabbage, goulash and stews; mixed with sour cream or cottage cheese; used also in cookies.

CARDAMOM: The plant grows in India and Mexico but will not thrive in the United States. The seeds are very aromatic and are used in buns, coffeecake, Danish pastry, cookies, with grape, grapefruit and orange salads, and in green pea soup.

CHERVIL: The lacy leaves have a taste similar to parsley and tarragon combined. They're used to flavor sauces, fish and shell-fish, in cream soups (pea, asparagus), in omelets, cottage cheese, with roast lamb or any cooked greens.

CHIVES: The delicate tubular leaves have a very mild onion flavor and are valuable in cottage cheese, sour cream sauce, omelets. Other favorite uses are chives stirred into a butter sauce and poured over fresh asparagus, sprinkled over broiled tomatoes and in tomato aspic.

CORIANDER: This plant is native to Europe and Asia, and while not well known in America as yet, makes a valuable addition to Italian dishes, sausage, stuffing for wild game and poultry. The flavor resembles cumin and caraway. The seeds when powdered make a superb gravy (add ¼ teaspoon to 2 cups of liquid). Used in sweet pickles. Try just one seed crushed in the bottom of a cup of espresso, Irish coffee or a demitasse—unique.

CUMIN: This herb is cultivated for commercial use in Africa, Europe and Mexico; the seeds add a nutty flavor to cheeses, rye bread, deviled eggs, meat loaf, rice, in Mexican dishes, and in some of the milder dips for appetizers.

DILL: Most important to flavor tossed salads, potato salad, pickles, cabbage, turnips, cottage cheese, seafood cocktail sauces, tartar sauce; use in bean or cream of tomato soup, and with beets or cauliflower.

FENNEL, SWEET: The leaves have a mild licorice flavor. They are used in cream sauces, salads, clear soups and broths, and as a garnish. If the roots of fennel are allowed to grow to about the size of an egg, they're delicious cooked and eaten with a butter sauce, a famous delicacy in Florence and Naples.

GARLIC: Used sparingly, this herb is distinctive in vegetable and meat soups, tossed green salads, spaghetti sauces, in all Italian and Mexican dishes, on French bread, in pickles and in salad dressings as well as in meat casseroles.

HORSERADISH: This herb is easy to grow but the process of grating or grinding is a "tearful" task—easier to buy the fresh ground horseradish at the market. Good mixed with mustard or mayonnaise for a meat and fish sauce, in cocktail sauces, and is a special treat on hot or cold beef tongue. The flavor is sharp and hot.

LEEKS: These wide, flat-leaved plants are grown extensively in England and Wales, as well as in southern Europe. They're grown in trenches covered with straw to make them tender and to bleach the tops. Very mild in flavor, similar to chives, the chopped leaves are excellent in tossed green salads, baked potatoes, chicken soup and mixed with most boiled or braised vegetables.

LOVAGE: The fresh celery flavor makes this herb useful in fish chowders, tossed green salads, soups and stews, or the leaves and stems can be cooked as celery is cooked.

MARJORAM, SWEET: This versatile little plant has many uses; the leaves add much to egg dishes, baked or broiled fish, rubbed on both beef and pork roasts, in salads, and vegetables, especially carrots and all the squash family. Marjoram is mildly spicy and pungent.

MINTS: There are many varieties, the most popular of which are apple mint, pineapple mint, orange mint, lemon mint, spearmint and peppermint. All are good in fruit salads, iced beverages, applesauce, baked apples, jellies, with green peas, as herb vinegars, with cooked cabbage or coleslaw, in cream cheese, and they make delightful herb teas—brisk, refreshing taste, hot or cold; they're most attractive as garnishes.

MUSTARD: We use mustard in three forms: the fresh green leaves (mustard greens), the dried seeds whole in pickles, and the powdered seed in salad mustard as a peppery spread or sauce, and in certain recipes. The tender young greens grow all over the United States; mustard is grown commercially for seed in California.

NASTURTIUM: An herb? Yes, indeed! The bright green round leaves are delicious used in place of lettuce or watercress for sandwiches; they have a sharp, distinctive taste. Allow the seeds to ripen and use in all types of pickles, or pickle the seeds in brine and use as a substitute for capers.

ORÉGANO: This plant, frequently called wild marjoram, has a strong aromatic flavor and is valuable in all Italian and Mexican dishes, in sausage, poultry stuffing, with stewed tomatoes, zucchini, squash and green salads. Try sprinkling crumbled orégano on chicken while it's frying—you'll like it.

PAPRIKA: The sweet red pepper dried and powdered makes this seasoning; it's grown commercially throughout the Mediterranean. The flavor depends largely on the amount used. It's good in all kinds of appetizers, in welsh rarebit, scrambled eggs, on broiled fish, in vegetable salads and salad dressings, cream sauces, with any vegetable and as a colorful garnish sprinkled on any main dish.

PARSLEY: There's hardly anything to which parsley doesn't add color and flavor, and it's also rich in vitamin C. Use as a garnish in soups, stews, salads, cottage and cream cheese, omelets, sauces, potatoes, all meats and poultry, all vegetables.

POPPY SEED: They add to the delicate taste of cookies and cakes, in canapés mixed with cheese, in fruit and vegetable salads, in cream sauces, with peas and sweet potatoes.

ROSE GERANIUM: There are really many varieties of scented geraniums including apple, mint, clove, walnut, filbert, lemon, orange, pineapple, lime, cinnamon, nutmeg and almond. The leaves of any of these are delicious in cookies and cakes, fruit salads, jellies and teas. Each variety has its own fruit or nut flavor.

ROSEMARY: Fresh or dried, the leaf of this herb has a personality all its own. Use in soups, stews, on roasts and meats of all kinds, in poultry stuffing, on game, with fried potatoes, broiled mushrooms, and sprinkled over rolls or biscuits before baking.

SAFFRON: This herb is grown in Europe and Asia. The yellow powder comes from the dried stigmas of a species of crocus. It takes 75,000 blossoms to produce 1 pound of saffron; the blooms must be hand-picked. It's therefore relatively expensive, but it's worth it. It's very special in fish soups, chicken casseroles, with rice, in cakes and cookies, and is a great favorite for French, Italian and Spanish dishes because of its rich, sweet taste.

SAGE: Most of us think of sage as merely the main herb in poultry stuffing; actually it's quite a versatile herb. The flavor is pungent and slightly bitter. Try it in meat and vegetable soups, stews, sausage, with soft cheeses, roast meats, meat loaf. Outstanding when used sparingly in eggplant dishes, on lima beans and with baked or boiled onions.

SAVORY: The narrow leaves of this plant have a tangy, meaty flavor. Good in vegetable juice cocktails, egg dishes, hamburgers and meat loaf, chicken or ham croquettes, in poultry stuffing, meat and vegetable soups, and performs miracles when cooked with green beans.

SESAME: The only part of sesame that is used is the seed—but what a difference sesame seeds make sprinkled on rolls, bread and cookies; toast the seeds and use as a garnish on fish, meat, chicken, soups and salads. Vegetables are improved with a dash of toasted sesame seed too. Has a slightly sweet, nutty taste.

SHALLOTS: This broad-leafed member of the onion family is grown commercially in England, France and Switzerland. It must be grown in greenhouses in the United States. Chopped fresh shallots are perfect in butter, cream or wine sauces, with most vegetables, sprinkled on broiled steaks and chops and in green salads.

SORREL: Also known as sour grass, this little plant with its shield-shaped leaves grows wild throughout the United States. The leaves are ready to eat at the same time as dandelion greens and should be harvested in the same manner. It's good cooked alone as greens or in combination with other green vegetables; adds a tang to salads, soups and omelets.

TARRAGON, FRENCH: Be sure to use the true French tarragon, as the other common type—Russian—is bitter and inedible. Fresh or dried, the leaves of this herb are most delicate and aniselike in flavor. Good with all fish and fish sauces, in salads, mustard, mayonnaise, tartar sauce, vinegar, egg dishes; in chicken or mushroom soup; extra fine on chicken cooked any way.

THYME: There are several varieties of thyme—English, golden, lemon, silver, caraway and creeping. All are good additions to seafood cocktails, sharp cheeses, fish chowders, with roasts and game, poultry, in tossed or molded vegetable salads and dressings, tomato sauces, stews, roasts, with potatoes, beans and onions.

The Difference Between Herbs and Spices

Much confusion exists concerning the distinction between herbs and spices. There are some simple rules to help classify the two. Herbs usually grow in the Northern Hemisphere, and the parts used are the leaves, roots, flowers and seeds. Spices almost always grow in the Southern Hemisphere and the parts used are the nuts, fruits, seeds and bark. The most popular spices are allspice, cinnamon, cloves, curry, ginger, nutmeg, pepper and turmeric.

How to Make Your Own Herb Blends and Vinegars

If you cook with herbs, you probably buy the herb blends found in supermarkets and gourmet food stores. You can easily make your own blends at home for much less than the price of the commercial products.

The recipes given here are for dried herbs, but if you grow your own plants and want fresh blends, multiply the amounts of herbs by four. Fresh blends cannot be kept for any length of time, but they can be frozen for later use.

Simply put the ingredients in a blender if you have one, and set at lowest speed. If you don't have a blender, crumble the dried herbs between your hands, then force them through a coarse strainer, or rub them over a piece of window screening cut to fit one of your mixing bowls. If fresh herbs are used for any of the blends, do not use a blender; chop very fine with mincer or cut with shears.

Herb wine vinegars are delicious and so useful—and easy to make, once you know how. They add immeasurably to the flavor and aroma of salads and dressings; they're a great addition to sweet-and-sour sauces, cabbage, broccoli, Brussels sprouts, spinach or any other dish which is improved with a dash of vinegar.

Mint Wine Vinegar is best for Harvard beets. Chive, Dill and Garlic Wine Vinegars blend well in oil-and-vinegar dressings; Basil and Tarragon Wine Vinegars are versatile and can be used with almost any vegetable or green salad. Burnet Wine Vinegar, if you can find or grow burnet, is superb in potato salad and seafood salads.

Herb wine vinegars must be made with fresh green herbs. These are not too difficult to find, or they can be grown easily in your garden or a kitchen window box. Garlic cloves are available at almost all markets, and dill is found in stores in late summer. Basil, burnet, chives, tarragon and mint do well in a sunny spot in a long planter if you have no garden space. (See Growing Herbs in Your Garden for growing information.)

Red and white wine vinegar can usually be found in gourmet shops, but even easier and less expensive is to make them yourself. Use equal parts of chianti, burgundy, or whatever red wine you like, with a good cider vinegar. For the white wine vinegars, use equal parts of Rhine, sauterne, or any favorite white wine, with a good quality white vinegar.

HERB SALT

Just a dash of this blend will add interest to most meat dishes

¼ c. parsley flakes	1 tblsp. paprika
1 tblsp. dried basil leaves	1 tsp. celery flakes
1 tblsp. dried orégano leaves	1 c. salt

With your blender set at lowest speed, sprinkle the parsley, basil, orégano, paprika and celery flakes into blender a little at a time. Add salt a little at a time and allow mixture to blend until the herbs are as fine as the salt. Pour into a shaker. Makes about 1 cup.

SALAD HERBS

Good on tossed salads, stewed tomatoes, winter squash and soups

¼ c. parsley flakes	1 tblsp. dried dill weed
¼ c. dried tarragon leaves	1 tblsp. celery flakes
1 tblsp. dried orégano leaves	

With blender set at lowest speed, sprinkle the parsley, tarragon, orégano, dill and celery flakes into blender a little at a time and allow to blend for 5 seconds after each addition. Place in airtight container. Use ½ tsp. for 4 servings. Makes ½ cup.

SAVORY MEAT BLEND

Seven herbs in this one—perfect for poultry and roasts

1 tblsp. dried summer savory leaves	1 tblsp. dried thyme leaves
¼ c. parsley flakes	1 tblsp. dried basil leaves
1 tblsp. dried orégano leaves	1 tblsp. dried sage leaves
1 tblsp. dried marjoram leaves	1 tsp. onion salt

With blender set at lowest speed, sprinkle savory, parsley, orégano, marjoram, thyme, basil, sage and onion salt into blender a little at a time and allow to blend for 5 seconds after each addition. Place in airtight container. Use ½ tsp. for 4 servings. Makes ⅓ cup.

FINES HERBES

Perk up the most ordinary soups and stews with this herb blend

1 tblsp. grated lemon rind	1 tsp. dried marjoram leaves
1 tblsp. parsley flakes	1 tsp. dried basil leaves
1 tblsp. dried tarragon leaves	1 tsp. celery salt

With blender set at lowest speed, sprinkle grated lemon rind, parsley, tarragon, marjoram, basil and celery salt into blender a little at a time and allow to blend for 5 seconds after each addition. Place in airtight container. Use ½ tsp. for 4 servings. Makes 3 tablespoons.

BOUQUET GARNI

A French chef's blend that's marvelous for fish and shellfish

1 tblsp. parsley flakes	1 tsp. dried tarragon leaves
1 tblsp. onion flakes	1 tsp. dried basil leaves
1 tblsp. celery flakes	

With blender set at lowest speed, sprinkle parsley, onion flakes, celery flakes, tarragon and basil into blender a little at a time. Blend for 5 seconds after each addition. Place in airtight container. Use ½ tsp. for 4 servings. Makes 2 tablespoons.

HERB MUSTARD

Use this zippy mustard and it soon will become a family favorite

2 c. prepared mustard	1 tsp. dried orégano leaves,
¼ c. parsley flakes, crumbled	crumbled
2 tblsp. dried tarragon leaves,	1 tsp. dried basil leaves,
crumbled	crumbled
1 tsp. dried dill weed	¼ c. cider vinegar

Pour mustard into large mixing bowl. Add parsley, tarragon, dill, orégano and basil. Mix thoroughly. Gradually stir in vinegar. Place in covered jar and refrigerate. Let stand for 2 or 3 days to allow herbs to flavor mustard. Makes 2 cups.

HERB BUTTER

Delicious on French bread, rolls, baked potatoes and meat

1 lb. butter or regular	1 tblsp. dried tarragon leaves,
margarine	crumbled
2 tblsp. chopped fresh parsley	1 tblsp. chopped fresh or
1 tblsp. dried basil leaves,	frozen chives
crumbled	

Place butter in large mixing bowl and let stand at room temperature until soft. Add parsley, basil, tarragon and chives and mix thoroughly with electric mixer. Pack into a container with a tight cover and let stand overnight for flavor to develop. Makes 1 pound.

HERB MARINADE

This marinade keeps for weeks—good on meats and poultry

1 c. red wine vinegar	1 tsp. dried tarragon leaves,
½ c. olive oil or salad oil	crumbled
¼ c. lemon juice	1 tsp. salt
1 tblsp. onion flakes	1 tsp. black pepper
2 tblsp. sugar	1 tsp. paprika
1 tsp. dried orégano leaves,	½ tsp. Worcestershire sauce
crumbled	

Pour wine vinegar into blender jar. Add oil, lemon juice, onion flakes, sugar, orégano, tarragon, salt, pepper, paprika and Worcestershire sauce. Blend at low speed for 5 to 10 seconds. Pour into bottle or jar with a tight cover and store in refrigerator.

If you don't have a blender, shake mixture thoroughly in a jar. Makes 1¾ cups.

BASIL WINE VINEGAR

Pour vinegar into attractive bottles and give as hostess gifts

1½ c. Rhine, sauterne or other	1½ c. white vinegar
white wine	2 c. fresh young basil leaves

Place wine and vinegar in saucepan over low heat. Bring to scalding, but do not boil.

Meanwhile, wash and clean basil, and place in a sterilized 1-qt. jar. Pour hot liquid slowly over basil. Seal tightly and store in a dark place for 3 weeks. Strain vinegar and put in smaller sterilized bottles, if desired. (Place a sprig of basil in each small bottle.) Makes 3 cups.

NOTE: You can substitute 3 c. white wine vinegar for the white wine and vinegar, if you like.

BURNET WINE VINEGAR

An unusual vinegar blend perfect for use in salad dressing

1½ c. Rhine, sauterne or other white wine

1½ c. white vinegar
2 c. fresh burnet leaves

Place wine and vinegar in saucepan over low heat. Bring to scalding, but do not boil.

Meanwhile, wash burnet thoroughly and place in a sterilized 1-qt. jar. Pour hot liquid slowly over burnet. Seal tightly and store in a dark place for 3 weeks. Strain and put in smaller sterilized bottles, if desired. Makes 3 cups.

NOTE: You can substitute 3 c. white wine vinegar for the white wine and vinegar, if you like.

CHIVE WINE VINEGAR

Keep this on your shelf and use in any of your favorite salads

1½ c. Rhine, sauterne or other white wine

1½ c. white vinegar
2 c. chopped fresh chives

Place wine and vinegar in saucepan over low heat. Bring to scalding, but do not boil.

Meanwhile, wash chives carefully, removing any flower stems or blossoms, and place in a sterilized 1-qt. jar. Pour hot liquid slowly over chives. Seal tightly and store in a dark place for 3 weeks. Strain and place in smaller sterilized bottles, if desired. Makes 3 cups.

NOTE: You can substitute 3 c. white wine vinegar for the white wine and vinegar, if you like.

DILL WINE VINEGAR

This vinegar enhances tuna salads and sandwich spreads

1½ c. Rhine, sauterne or other   1½ c. white vinegar
   white wine   20 umbels of dill

Place wine and vinegar in saucepan over low heat. Bring to scalding, but do not boil.

Meanwhile, wash dill carefully, removing any dead stems or coarse stalks, and cut in 1″ lengths. Place in a sterilized 1-qt. jar. Pour hot liquid slowly over dill. Seal tightly and store in a dark place for 3 weeks. Strain dill vinegar through cheesecloth to avoid cloudiness. Makes 3 cups.

NOTE: You can substitute 3 c. white wine vinegar for the white wine and vinegar, if you like.

GARLIC WINE VINEGAR

This sparkling garlic vinegar is useful in marinades and dressings

1 pt. chianti, burgundy or other   1 pt. cider vinegar
   red wine   1 bulb garlic

Place wine and vinegar in saucepan over low heat. Bring to scalding, but do not boil.

Meanwhile, remove outer skin from garlic bulb and break into cloves; peel each clove.

Remove liquid from heat; drop garlic cloves into liquid and let stand until lukewarm. Pour entire contents into a sterilized 1-qt. jar. Seal tightly and store in a dark place for 3 weeks. Strain before using. Makes 1 quart.

NOTE: You can substitute 1 qt. red wine vinegar for the red wine and cider vinegar, if you like.

MINT WINE VINEGAR

Lamb dishes will be greatly improved with this vinegar

1½ c. chianti, burgundy or   1½ c. cider vinegar
   other red wine   2 c. fresh mint leaves

Place wine and vinegar in saucepan over low heat. Bring to scalding, but do not boil.

Meanwhile, wash mint thoroughly, and place in a sterilized 1-qt. jar. Pour hot liquid slowly over mint. Seal tightly and store in a dark place for 3 weeks. Strain and place in smaller sterilized bottles, if desired. Makes 3 cups.

NOTE: Any variety of mint can be used. You can substitute 3 c. red wine vinegar for the red wine and cider vinegar, if you like.

TARRAGON WINE VINEGAR

Adds zip to both chicken and seafood salads

1½ c. chianti, burgundy or   1½ c. cider vinegar
   other red wine   2 c. fresh tarragon leaves

Place wine and vinegar in saucepan over low heat. Bring to scalding, but do not boil.

Meanwhile, carefully wash tarragon and place in a sterilized 1-qt. jar. Slowly pour hot liquid over tarragon. Seal tightly and store in a dark place for 3 weeks. Strain and place in smaller sterilized bottles, if desired, adding a bunch of tarragon to each. Makes 3 cups.

NOTE: You can substitute 3 c. red wine vinegar for the red wine and cider vinegar, if you like.

Appetizers, Canapés and Hors d'Oeuvres

Experimentation is the art and heart of herb cookery—and appetizers are the perfect subjects for your taste-tests. When you prepare before-dinner nibbles or drinks, you can afford to let yourself go, using herbs generously. With appetites piqued, your guests and family will want to know, "What makes this taste so good?"

All fruit and vegetable juices make perfect preludes to a good meal. Try pineapple juice with a sprig of one of the mints, or sauerkraut juice so cold it's a frozen mush, topped with a sprig of basil. For a shivery winter evening, a mug of piping hot tomato juice sprinkled with a pinch of dill is warming and delicious.

The before-dinner drink and snack gives everyone a chance to let down, relax and get ready to enjoy the meal you've prepared. Don't limit this service to just the guest evenings! A small nibble is easy to set out and your family's best conversations are likely to start over a platter of cheese and toast rounds.

This chapter contains many fresh ideas for doctoring cheese spreads and concocting dips, but soon you'll be thinking of your own combinations. You'll also want to try some special treats for company. The Walnut Cheese Balls are a surprise package, and the Prosciutto and Orégano Squares are ideal for a buffet—you can keep them hot on a warming tray.

You have an abundant choice of breads to serve with these herb spreads. Sample them all—French bread, pumpernickel, light and dark rye, salt-rising, date-and-nut, brown bread, cheese bread. Sliced thin and cut into different shapes, breads add eye appeal to your platters. And don't pass by cheese sticks, bread sticks, croutons, pretzels, potato chips and corn chips—any of which you can spread or dip. To say nothing of the crackers

. . . round, square, triangular; salty, cheese-flavored, sprinkled with sesame, caraway or poppy seeds . . . the choice is endless.

HERBED CLAM DIP

Serve with chips and assorted crackers for a delicious snack

1 (3 oz.) pkg. cream cheese
1 c. dairy sour cream
1 (10½ oz.) can minced clams, drained
1 tblsp. minced onion
½ tsp. garlic powder
½ tsp. dried basil leaves, crumbled
¼ tsp. salt
$\frac{1}{16}$ tsp. ground red pepper
1 tblsp. lemon juice

Soften cream cheese at room temperature, then blend with sour cream. Add clams, onion, garlic powder, basil, salt, red pepper and lemon juice; mix thoroughly. Chill until serving time. Makes 2 cups.

HERBED SOUR CREAM DIP

Good with celery, carrots, cherry tomatoes and zucchini sticks

½ c. dairy sour cream
¼ c. mayonnaise
⅛ tsp. garlic powder
⅛ tsp. onion salt
$\frac{1}{16}$ tsp. pepper
$\frac{1}{16}$ tsp. ground red pepper
¼ tsp. dried basil leaves, crumbled
¼ tsp. salt
Paprika

Combine sour cream, mayonnaise, garlic powder, onion salt, pepper, red pepper, basil and salt; mix thoroughly. Chill. At serving time, place in bowl and garnish with paprika. Makes about ¾ cup.

WALNUT CHEESE BALLS

Spear small cheese balls with a toothpick for easier serving

1 (8 oz.) pkg. cream cheese
½ c. crumbled blue cheese
½ tsp. dried basil leaves, finely
   crumbled

2 tblsp. dairy sour cream
½ tsp. dried dill weed, finely
   crumbled
½ c. chopped walnuts

Let cream cheese and blue cheese stand at room temperature until soft, then blend together until smooth. Add basil, sour cream and dill; mix thoroughly. Chill.

Form chilled mixture into small balls or one large ball if you like. Roll in chopped nuts. Chill until serving time. Makes 1¼ cups cheese mixture.

HERBED CHEESE SPREAD

Made in a blender in no time; this spread is extra good

1 (8 oz.) pkg. cream cheese
½ c. crumbled blue cheese

2 to 3 tsp. Salad Herbs (see
   Index)

Let cream cheese and blue cheese stand at room temperature until soft, then blend together until smooth. Add Salad Herbs, and mix well. Chill until serving time. Makes 1¼ cups.

CREOLE SPREAD

Keep handy to serve on toast rounds or crackers. Men especially like the way herbs blend with dried beef and cream cheese

1 (8 oz.) pkg. cream cheese
½ c. dried beef
1 tblsp. mayonnaise

1 tsp. prepared horseradish
1 tsp. chili sauce
½ tsp. Salad Herbs (see Index)

Soften cream cheese at room temperature. Beat until smooth.

Finely shred dried beef; mix with cream cheese. Add mayonnaise, horseradish, chili sauce and Salad Herbs; mix thoroughly. Store in refrigerator. Makes 1¼ cups.

TEA SPREAD

Crunchiness and the good flavor of parsley make this special. Serve it on brown bread at your next tea or club meeting

1 (8 oz.) pkg. cream cheese
¼ c. crunchy peanut butter
2 tblsp. grape jelly
2 tblsp. lemon juice
2 tsp. parsley flakes, finely crumbled

Soften cream cheese at room temperature. Combine with peanut butter, jelly, lemon juice and parsley; beat with electric mixer until smooth. Chill until serving time. Makes 1½ cups.

CRABMEAT CANAPÉS

Herb Mustard and Herb Salt add zip to crabmeat. For variety, add chopped celery to mixture and serve on lettuce

1 (7½ oz.) can crabmeat, drained
1 tblsp. mayonnaise
1 tblsp. Herb Mustard (see Index)
¼ tsp. Herb Salt (see Index)
Toast rounds or crackers
1 (4 oz.) can sliced mushrooms, drained
1 tsp. paprika

Flake crabmeat, then mash with a fork. Mix with mayonnaise, Herb Mustard and Herb Salt.

Spread mixture on toast rounds or crackers. Garnish each with a mushroom slice and sprinkle with paprika. Makes about 1 cup spread.

OLD-FASHIONED SAGE CHEESE

Cottage cheese and cream cheese, accented with sage, take on a new personality in this canapé spread—try it for a change

1 (3 oz.) pkg. cream cheese	¼ tsp. salt
1 c. creamed cottage cheese	⅛ tsp. pepper
2 tblsp. crumbled Roquefort cheese	⅛ tsp. garlic powder
	½ tsp. lemon juice
2½ tsp. ground sage	Paprika or parsley flakes

Soften cream cheese at room temperature, then combine with cottage and Roquefort cheeses; mix thoroughly. Add sage, salt, pepper, garlic powder and lemon juice. Mix well. Chill 2 to 3 hours, or until serving time. Garnish with paprika. Makes 1½ cups.

TUNA TRIANGLES

Garnish each triangle with a small slice of spicy dill pickle

1 (9¼ oz.) can water-pack tuna, drained	¼ c. creamed cottage cheese
2 tblsp. mayonnaise	1 tsp. Salad Herbs (see Index)
¼ c. chopped pimiento-stuffed olives	Toast triangles
	Chopped fresh parsley

Mash and shred tuna with a fork. Combine tuna with mayonnaise, olives, cottage cheese and Salad Herbs in blender set at lowest speed for 10 to 15 seconds, or until mixture is smooth.

Remove from blender and chill. Serve on toast triangles, and garnish with parsley. Makes 1½ cups.

POOR MAN'S PÂTÉ

Herb Mustard is the secret ingredient that adds the special zest

1 (8 oz.) pkg. cream cheese
1 c. mashed liverwurst (about ½ lb.)
1 tblsp. Herb Mustard (see Index)
½ tsp. Worcestershire sauce
½ c. fresh or frozen chopped chives
1 tsp. dried marjoram leaves, crumbled

Soften cream cheese at room temperature, then combine with liverwurst in small bowl and mix with electric mixer at medium speed. Add Herb Mustard, Worcestershire sauce, chives and marjoram; continue to beat until smooth. Chill several hours, or overnight before serving. Makes about 2 cups.

NOTE: This spicy pâté is especially good served on melba toast. Try it on toasted rye bread squares and plain crackers too.

CELERY HERB WHEELS

You'll receive raves when you serve these crisp herbed appetizers

1 bunch celery
1½ c. Homemade Pimiento Cheese (see Index)

Separate celery branches and wash carefully. Cut off all leaves. Fill each celery branch with Homemade Pimiento Cheese. Press branches back together in a bunch.

Wrap firmly in plastic wrap or foil and refrigerate several hours, or overnight. To serve, cut in thin crosswise slices. Makes about 1 dozen wheels.

NOTE: If you do not have the Homemade Pimiento Cheese, you can substitute 1½ c. pimiento cheese spread mixed with 1 tsp. Salad Herbs (see Index), if you like.

PROSCIUTTO AND ORÉGANO SQUARES

Keep these hot on a warming tray throughout the entire party

Pastry for 1-crust pie	1 tsp. sugar
2 tblsp. water	½ tsp. dill seeds
2 tblsp. instant minced onion	½ tsp. dried orégano leaves
½ c. shredded carrots	½ tsp. celery salt
¾ c. finely chopped seeded tomatoes	⅛ tsp. pepper
	1 egg, well beaten
¼ c. finely chopped prosciutto	1 thin slice prosciutto

Roll out pastry ⅛″ thick; line an 8″ square baking pan, allowing pastry to come up only ¾″ on sides.

Add water to instant minced onion and set aside for 10 minutes.

Blend together carrots, tomatoes, chopped prosciutto, sugar, dill, orégano, celery salt and pepper; stir in softened onion. Spoon mixture into pastry-lined pan. Pour beaten egg over top.

Cut prosciutto slice in ½″ squares and arrange over top of pie. Bake in hot oven (425°) 10 minutes. Reduce heat to moderate (350°) and bake 30 minutes longer, or until crust is lightly browned and filling is firm in center. Remove from oven and cool thoroughly. Cut in 2″ squares and serve as an appetizer. Makes 16 squares.

Variation

Ham and Orégano Squares: Substitute ¼ c. finely chopped boiled ham for the prosciutto in the pie filling, and cut 1 thin slice boiled ham in ½″ squares for top instead of the prosciutto squares.

STUFFED MUSHROOMS

This hot appetizer is certain to be popular at your next party

1 lb. large fresh mushrooms
1 c. soft bread crumbs
½ c. chopped prosciutto
¾ c. canned Italian plum
   tomatoes, drained
1 tblsp. parsley flakes
⅟₁₆ tsp. garlic powder
½ tsp. dried orégano leaves

¼ tsp. pepper
2½ tblsp. grated Parmesan
   or Romano cheese
1 tblsp. olive oil
¼ c. lemon juice
¼ c. olive oil
¼ c. water

Remove stems from mushrooms. Wash and dry caps and set aside.

Combine bread crumbs, prosciutto, tomatoes, parsley, garlic powder, orégano, pepper, cheese and 1 tblsp. olive oil; blend well.

Dip each mushroom cap in lemon juice, then fill with about 1 heaping teaspoonful of crumb mixture. Arrange mushrooms in shallow baking dish or pie pan. Sprinkle with ¼ c. olive oil. Pour water in bottom of pan to prevent mushrooms from becoming too dry.

Bake in hot oven (400°) 15 minutes, or until mushrooms are browned and heated throughout. Serve immediately. Makes 6 servings.

Savory Soups

Whether you heat a quick can of soup for lunch, or simmer your own recipe for hours on the back burner, you can—and should—take advantage of herbs to develop flavor.

If you're serving a canned soup, depend on this one quick trick: In the bottom of each cup or bowl, put just a pinch of any culinary herb, plus a teaspoon of sherry, then pour in the hot soup. Mmmm! The same old soup will have a different personality.

Try adding an herb bag to your favorite homemade soup. Cut a 4-inch square from cheesecloth, scraps of organdy or fine net. For each quart of soup, place ¼ teaspoon of Salad Herbs, Savory Meat Blend or Bouquet Garni (see Index for these 3 recipes) in the center of the square, bring up corners and tie. Drop into soup to simmer; remove the bag before serving.

To mince fresh herbs for soups, use kitchen shears, French chef's knife or a commercial mincer. The fresh herbs will remain in the soup so they should be very finely chopped.

Soups become much more appetizing and attractive when served with a garnish: a dab of whipped sour cream, toasted croutons, a sprinkling of Parmesan cheese, minced chives or chopped parsley, a slice of stuffed green olive, a tiny square of pimiento or green pepper, grated hard-cooked egg yolk, or a thin slice of lemon or lime.

Why forget about soups on hot days? Try Consommé Madrilene or Crème Vichyssoise with chives some warm evening and watch your family perk up for the next course.

IRISH BROTH

*The addition of Herb Salt gives this hearty soup character—
serve it piping hot with crackers on a frosty cold day*

2 tblsp. butter or regular margarine

1 lb. beef chuck, cut in ½″ cubes

2 qts. water

½ c. pearl barley

2 carrots, peeled and sliced

1 medium onion, finely chopped

1 c. shredded cabbage

4 beef bouillon cubes

½ tsp. salt

¼ tsp. pepper (optional)

1 tsp. Herb Salt (see Index)

Melt butter in 4-qt. saucepan. Add beef cubes and brown. Add water, barley, carrots, onion, cabbage, bouillon cubes and seasonings.

Bring to a boil; reduce heat, cover and simmer over low heat for 2 hours. Adjust seasonings, if desired. Makes 9 cups.

NOTE: Flavors blend better if soup is refrigerated overnight, reheated and served the next day.

GARBANZO BEAN SOUP

Chili powder and orégano team with chick-peas in this soup

1 (1 lb. 4 oz.) can garbanzo beans (chick-peas)

Water

¾ c. finely chopped green pepper

1 c. finely chopped onion

½ tsp. chili powder

¼ tsp. dried orégano leaves, finely crumbled

½ tsp. salt

⅛ tsp. pepper

Place garbanzos with their liquid in 3-qt. saucepan. Add 1 can of water. Add green pepper, onion, chili powder, orégano, salt and pepper; bring to a boil. Cover and cook over low heat until onion and green pepper are tender, about 30 minutes. Makes 3½ cups.

CHIVE CREAM SOUP

Will appeal especially to the woman who grows her own chives

2 tblsp. butter or regular
  margarine
1 c. finely chopped fresh chives
¼ c. finely chopped celery
¼ c. finely chopped fresh
  parsley

½ tsp. salt
2 c. light cream
Sour cream

Melt butter in small saucepan. Add chives, celery and parsley; sauté until tender.

Add salt and light cream, and bring just to a boil. Serve immediately, topping each serving with a dollop of sour cream. Makes about 2 cups.

CRÈME VICHYSSOISE

This famous soup contains chives both as an ingredient and an attractive garnish—you'll like the result. Serve it hot or icy cold

1 c. diced pared potatoes
1 c. finely chopped onion
2 tblsp. melted butter
1 (10½ oz.) can condensed
  cream of chicken soup

1 c. light cream
½ c. finely chopped fresh or
  frozen chives
½ tsp. salt
Chopped chives

Cook potatoes in boiling water until tender; drain.

Slowly cook onion in melted butter until tender, but do not brown. Place in blender container and blend. Add potatoes, soup, cream, ½ c. chives and salt; blend at high speed to purée vegetables.

Pour into saucepan. Heat through, and serve garnished with chopped chives. Makes 3½ cups.

NEW ENGLAND CLAM CHOWDER

An all-time favorite with a touch of thyme for added flavor

¼ lb. salt pork, diced
2 c. boiling water
3 c. diced pared potatoes
¼ c. instant minced onion
¼ tsp. salt
¼ tsp. pepper
18 fresh clams with liquid or
    4 (7½ oz.) cans minced
    clams, undrained

1 qt. hot milk
½ tsp. ground thyme
2 tblsp. butter or regular
    margarine

In 4-qt. saucepan fry salt pork until crisp. Add boiling water, potatoes, instant minced onion, salt and pepper. Cover and cook 10 to 12 minutes, until potatoes are almost tender.

If fresh clams are used, steam until shells open. Drain off liquid and reserve (you'll need about 1½ c.). Chop clams and add to saucepan; cook 5 minutes. Stir in clam liquid, milk, thyme and butter. If minced clams are used, stir in with milk, thyme and butter.

Cover and simmer 5 minutes, or until potatoes are tender. Makes about 3 quarts.

CRAB BISQUE

Complete the meal with a crisp salad and a fresh red apple

¼ c. onion flakes
¼ c. water
1 tblsp. butter
1 tblsp. flour
1 (6½ oz.) can crabmeat
Water
1 (1 lb.) can tomatoes in
    purée

1 tsp. salt
1 tsp. parsley flakes
1 small bay leaf
½ tsp. dried thyme leaves,
    crushed
⅛ tsp. garlic powder
⅛ tsp. pepper
⅛ tsp. ground red pepper

Combine onion flakes with ¼ c. water; let stand 8 minutes to soften.

Melt butter in medium saucepan. Add flour; stir until smooth and brown.

Drain crabmeat, reserving liquid. Add water to crab liquid to make 1½ c.; pour into saucepan. Add onion flakes, tomatoes, salt, parsley, bay leaf, thyme, garlic powder, pepper and red pepper; bring to a boil. Reduce heat and simmer 15 minutes, stirring occasionally.

Flake crabmeat and add to saucepan; cook 5 minutes longer. Remove bay leaf. Makes 3⅔ cups.

POTATO CHOWDER

A hearty soup that is easy to prepare for a hot luncheon treat

2 c. diced pared potatoes	⅛ tsp. pepper
½ c. sliced carrots	1 tsp. parsley flakes
2 tsp. salt	2 tblsp. flour
1 tblsp. instant minced onion	2 c. milk
2 c. boiling water	3 slices crisp-cooked bacon,
¼ tsp. ground sage	crumbled
¼ tsp. paprika	

Combine potatoes, carrots, salt, instant minced onion and boiling water in 2-qt. saucepan. Cover and cook until vegetables are tender, 10 to 15 minutes. Add sage, paprika, pepper and parsley.

Blend flour with ¼ c. milk until smooth. Add with remaining milk to vegetables, stirring constantly. Cook until slightly thickened, stirring occasionally. Serve garnished with bacon. Makes about 1 quart.

FRENCH ONION SOUP

The perfect choice for a first course for that special dinner

6 to 8 medium onions, chopped	½ tsp. salt
1 tblsp. butter or regular margarine	½ tsp. pepper
	¼ tsp. dried orégano leaves
1 (10½ oz.) can condensed beef consommé	½ tsp. parsley flakes
	Rusk rounds
2 c. water	½ c. Parmesan cheese

Place chopped onions and melted butter in 2-qt. saucepan and fry until onions are brown.

Add consommé, water, salt, pepper, orégano and parsley. Cover and simmer at least 2 hours.

To serve, place a rusk round in the bottom of each bowl; fill with soup. Sprinkle Parmesan cheese over top. Makes 4½ cups.

CONSOMMÉ MADRILENE

An adaptation of the French soup. It's seasoned with Basil Wine Vinegar and Herb Salt instead of tomato juice

2 (10½ oz.) cans condensed beef consommé	⅓ c. finely chopped celery
	¼ tsp. Herb Salt (see Index)
1 tsp. Basil Wine Vinegar (see Index) or white wine vinegar	Lime slices

Combine consommé, vinegar, celery and Herb Salt; mix well. Refrigerate until firm.

Stir consommé before serving. Serve with thin lime slice on top of each serving. Makes 2½ cups.

HERBED BUTTERMILK SOUP

A refreshing treat, especially during the hot summer months

2 (10½ oz.) cans condensed
    tomato soup
2 soup cans buttermilk
1 tsp. dried basil leaves,
    crumbled

½ tsp. sugar
¼ tsp. pepper
Dairy sour cream
Paprika

In a large mixing bowl combine soup, buttermilk, basil, sugar and pepper. Mix well and chill.

At serving time, spoon soup into bowls; top each serving with a dollop of sour cream and sprinkle with paprika. Makes 5 cups.

Herb Teas and Other Beverages

Herb tea bags can be made as easily as soup bags: Simply cut 4-inch squares of cheesecloth or fine net and place ¼ teaspoon of your favorite herb in the center. Bring up the corners and tie with sewing thread, leaving one end of the thread long enough to pull the bag out of the teapot. If you have a tea ball, place ¼ teaspoon of herb in that; place in a teapot and pour 2 cups of boiling water into the pot. Let steep as long as you would any ordinary tea, and remove the tea ball before pouring. Or, you can prepare herb tea the old-fashioned way: Rinse the teapot with hot water, pour ¼ teaspoon of an herb in the bottom, pour 2 cups of boiling water into the pot and let steep, then strain when you pour.

If you use ¼ teaspoon of any herb, it is enough for 2 cups; if you wish to add an herb to your regular tea, then you will need 4 cups of boiling water. For a distinctive and original flavor, add to your regular orange pekoe or green tea 1 clove bud, or 1 coriander seed; or, add to any herb tea ½-inch stick of cinnamon and just a pinch of grated orange rind.

You owe it to yourself to try herb teas, either hot or cold, for pure enjoyment as well as for their curative qualities. Here are some of the best flavor combinations:

Angelica Tea: Has a delicate flavor much like a combination of vanilla and rhubarb.

Anise Tea: A licorice flavor, yet much more delicate.

Camomile Tea: A delicate fresh apple flavor, very mildly sedative, good for headaches and insomnia.

Fennel Tea: Pungent, aromatic and spicy, somewhat like nutmeg.

Horehound Tea: An old remedy for coughs and bronchitis; rather bitter.

Lemon Balm Tea: Fresh lemon flavor, good mixed with regular tea.

Lemon Verbena Tea: Lemon-and-flower taste; use for indigestion.

Mint Tea: All the mints make excellent teas, for indigestion, nausea or seasickness. Fine with regular teas too.

Sage Tea: As a "blood tonic"; also for heat exhaustion.

Wintergreen Tea: Sharp, tangy mint and clove taste.

Try honey for sweetening in teas, and add a slice of lemon if you wish. Honey is good for you, and it seems to bring out the delicate flavors of the herb teas.

If you have a mint bed or lemon balm outside your kitchen door, you have the means to make any summer fruit drink look cooler. Mash one of the leaves to release the fresh aroma when you add sprigs to each tall glass. Carbonated beverages such as ginger ale, club soda or tonic water are perfect mixers for fruit juice bases. And a little wine will add flavor and body to most fruit mixtures.

DILLED TOMATO JUICE COCKTAIL

Serve hot in mugs or frosty cold—it's the perfect meal opener

1 (12 oz.) can tomato juice   1 tblsp. lemon juice
1 tsp. chopped fresh dill

Heat tomato juice to scalding. Pour over chopped dill; add lemon juice and refrigerate overnight.

Strain tomato juice and pour into glasses. Makes 4 servings. Double recipe for 8 servings.

NOTE: Juice also can be served hot. After refrigerating, reheat.

MULLED HERB WINE

A special treat on a cold night—sip slowly to savor the taste

1 c. boiling water	1 c. grape juice
¼ tsp. dried rosemary leaves, crushed	1 c. dry cocktail sherry
	1 (3″) stick cinnamon
½ tsp. mint flakes, crushed	4 or 5 whole cloves

Pour boiling water over rosemary and mint. Steep for 30 minutes. Strain; mix strained liquid with grape juice and sherry in saucepan. Place over low heat; add cinnamon and cloves, and simmer 10 minutes. Strain and serve hot in cups or mugs. Makes 4 servings. An easy recipe to double for 8 servings.

COFFEE CREAM FROST

You can serve this as a beverage or dessert—a real taste pleaser

2 tblsp. instant coffee	½ c. heavy cream, whipped
½ c. hot water	Fresh mint
1 qt. chocolate ice cream	

Dissolve instant coffee in hot water; let cool. Carefully fold chocolate ice cream into cooled coffee. Spoon into sherbet glasses and top with whipped cream. Garnish with mint leaves. Makes 6 servings.

ORANGE BREEZE

Serve in tall frosty glasses for a refreshing summer treat

3 c. orange juice	1 pt. orange sherbet, softened
2 tblsp. lemon juice	Orange slices
1 pt. vanilla ice cream, softened	Fresh mint

Pour orange and lemon juice in blender container. Spoon in ice cream and sherbet. Cover and blend on low speed until smooth. Pour into tall glasses over cracked ice. Garnish each with an orange slice and sprig of mint. Makes 6 servings.

CHOCOLATE SODA

Treat your children to a cooling ice cream soda this evening

1 (1 lb.) can chocolate syrup
½ c. light cream
2 pts. chocolate mint ice cream

2 qts. carbonated water
Fresh mint

Into each of 6 (12 oz.) glasses, pour 3 tblsp. chocolate syrup. Stir in 1 tblsp. light cream. Add 2 small scoops chocolate mint ice cream. Add carbonated water to fill each glass; stir lightly. Garnish with mint leaves. Serve immediately. Makes 6 servings.

LIME AND PINEAPPLE COOLER

Super summer drink . . . try with a cup of Rhine wine added

1 (46 oz.) can pineapple juice
1 tblsp. crushed fresh mint
    leaves
1 tblsp. crushed fresh lemon
    balm leaves

¼ c. lime juice
¼ c. sugar
1 (12 oz.) bottle club soda
Fresh mint

Heat pineapple juice and pour over mint and lemon balm leaves. Add lime juice and sugar. Steep for 30 minutes. Store in refrigerator until ready to serve.

Strain liquid and add club soda. Pour over crushed ice in tall glasses and garnish with a sprig of mint. Makes about ½ gallon.

Breads, Rolls and Muffins

Our grandmothers had time for breads "made from scratch," but most of us today have too many interests, errands and civic activities to spend all day in the kitchen. Prepared biscuit mixes and their relatives are a real blessing. With the addition of eggs, or cream, and an herb for your special touch, they fool even the most expert gourmet. Prepared yeast-roll mixes are so easy to use and the results most satisfactory.

Herbs that blend well with breads of all types are caraway seeds, poppy seeds, sesame seeds, aniseeds, parsley, rosemary, sage, savory, thyme and marjoram. In sweet rolls you may use mint, lemon balm or any scented geranium.

Almost any kind of bread or rolls will be improved with a serving of Herb Butter (see Index). Herb Butter is easy to make, keeps as well as plain butter or margarine, and is delicious on anything except your breakfast toast. Try it on leftover biscuits: Split them, spread with Herb Butter, sprinkle with grated cheese and run under the broiler long enough to melt the cheese.

Save leftover bread and rolls; slice and place them in a very slow oven to dry them out thoroughly. Then you can make bread crumbs and bottle them for later use. Or, cut dried bread into 1" cubes and save for croutons—you'll always have these on hand when you're busy.

POULTRY SEASONING CORN BREAD

Complement your next roast chicken dinner with this corn bread

1 c. sifted flour	½ tsp. poultry seasoning
1 c. cornmeal	1 egg
2 tsp. baking powder	1 c. sour milk
½ tsp. baking soda	⅓ c. water
½ tsp. salt	¼ c. shortening, melted

Combine flour, cornmeal, baking powder, soda, salt and poultry seasoning. Add egg, sour milk and water; mix just to moisten dry ingredients. Stir in shortening; do not overmix. Pour into hot, well-greased 8″ square baking pan.

Bake in hot oven (425°) 30 minutes, or until done. Serve hot, cut in squares. Makes 9 servings.

NOTE: To sour the milk, pour 1 tblsp. vinegar into a 1-c. measuring cup; fill with sweet milk. Let stand a few minutes before using.

HUSH PUPPIES

Traditionally served with fried fish—also good with chicken

1 c. cornmeal	½ c. buttermilk
2 tblsp. flour	¼ c. milk
1 tsp. salt	½ tsp. parsley flakes, finely
1 tsp. baking powder	crumbled
¼ tsp. baking soda	2 tblsp. finely minced onion
2 eggs, well beaten	Salad oil

Sift together cornmeal, flour, salt, baking powder and soda.

Combine eggs, buttermilk and milk. Add to dry ingredients, stirring just enough to moisten. Add parsley and onion. Let stand 15 minutes.

Drop by teaspoonfuls into hot oil (375°) 1″ deep. Fry, turning once, until hush puppies are puffed and golden brown on all sides. Drain on paper towels and serve hot. Makes 30.

SOUTHERN SPOON BREAD

Basil-seasoned soft bread—serve very hot with butter

1½ c. hot water	1 tsp. sugar
1 c. cornmeal	¼ tsp. dried basil leaves, finely
3 tblsp. melted butter or	crumbled
regular margarine	1 tsp. baking powder
3 egg yolks, slightly beaten	¼ tsp. baking soda
1 c. buttermilk	3 egg whites, stiffly beaten
1 tsp. salt	

Pour hot water into cornmeal, stirring constantly to keep from lumping. Add melted butter and egg yolks; stir until well blended. Stir in buttermilk, then salt, sugar, basil, baking powder and soda. Fold in egg whites. Pour into greased 2-qt. baking dish.

Bake in moderate oven (375°) 30 to 45 minutes. Bread is too soft to slice so serve with a spoon. Makes 4 to 6 servings.

CHIVE SPOON BREAD

A light and delicate bread that is especially good with butter

1 qt. milk	1½ tsp. salt
1 c. cornmeal	1 tsp. sugar
2 tblsp. chopped fresh or	1 tsp. baking powder
frozen chives	4 eggs, well beaten
2 tblsp. butter	

Scald milk in top of double boiler. Gradually stir in cornmeal and chives; cook until thickened.

Add butter, salt, sugar and baking powder. Gradually add hot mixture to eggs, stirring constantly. Pour into greased 2-qt. casserole.

Bake in hot oven (425°) 45 minutes. Serve at once. Bread is too soft to slice so serve with a spoon. Makes 6 to 8 servings.

DILLY CORN MUFFINS

Try these with your next tuna casserole luncheon—so delicious

¾ c. milk	1 egg, slightly beaten
1 tsp. dried dill weed	1 (12 oz.) pkg. corn muffin mix

Combine milk and dill weed in small saucepan. Scald milk; cool to lukewarm.

Stir egg into lukewarm milk mixture. Blend into corn muffin mix, stirring with a fork until blended (batter will be slightly lumpy). Spoon batter into well-greased muffin-pan cups, filling half full. Bake in hot oven (400°) 15 minutes. Serve piping hot. Makes 1 dozen.

SEASONED CORN STRIPS

Poultry seasoning added to the mix makes the flavor difference

1 (10 oz.) pkg. corn bread mix   1 egg
⅔ c. milk   ½ tsp. poultry seasoning

Combine corn bread mix, milk, egg and poultry seasoning; mix just enough to moisten dry ingredients. Pour batter into greased 8″ square baking pan.

Bake in hot oven (400°) 20 to 25 minutes or until golden brown. Cut in strips and serve warm with butter. Makes 16 strips.

SAVORY CORN MUFFINS

Summer savory gives these made-from-a-mix muffins just the right flavor—serve them with chicken or veal

1 (8½ oz.) pkg. corn muffin   1 egg
  mix (1⅔ c.)   ¼ tsp. dried summer savory,
⅓ c. milk   finely crumbled

Combine corn muffin mix, milk, egg and savory; mix just enough to moisten dry ingredients. Spoon batter into greased muffin-pan cups, filling half full.

Bake in hot oven (400°) 20 minutes. Makes 8 muffins.

POPPY SEED CRESCENTS

Attractive, yet so easy to prepare—a treat for any Sunday dinner

1 (13¾ oz.) pkg. hot roll mix   ¼ c. poppy seeds
2 tblsp. milk

Prepare roll mix according to package directions. Let rise in warm place until doubled. Punch down. On a lightly floured board, knead dough until smooth.

Divide dough in half. On lightly floured board roll each half into an 8″ circle. Cut each circle into 8 pie-shaped wedges. Starting from base of wedge, roll up; turn ends in slightly to form a crescent. Place on lightly greased baking sheet. Brush lightly with milk and sprinkle with poppy seeds. Cover and let rise in warm place until doubled, about 15 minutes.

Bake in hot oven (400°) 12 to 15 minutes, or until golden. Makes 16 crescents.

Variation

Poppy Seed Brioches: Prepare dough as directed for Poppy Seed Crescents, but instead of rolling dough in circles, cut it in 16 equal parts. Cut a third off each part. Shape small and larger portions into balls, and press a small ball into top of each larger ball. Place on lightly greased baking sheets. Brush lightly with milk and sprinkle with poppy seeds. Cover and let rise in warm place until doubled, about 15 minutes. Bake in moderate oven (375°) 12 minutes, or until golden brown. Makes 16.

HERB-FROSTED CURRANT ROLLS

Just the right touch of anise in frosting makes these a favorite

1 (13¾ oz.) pkg. hot roll mix	¾ c. confectioners sugar
6 tblsp. sugar	½ tsp. aniseeds
½ c. currants or raisins	1 tblsp. lemon juice
1 egg, well beaten	

Prepare roll mix according to package directions, but adding sugar and currants with the egg to yeast. Cover and let rise in warm place until light and doubled, 30 to 45 minutes.

On a floured board, roll or pat dough to 1″ thickness. Cut with floured 2″ biscuit cutter; place rolls on well-greased baking sheet. Cover and let rise again in warm place until doubled, 35 to 40 minutes.

Bake in moderate oven (375°) 20 to 30 minutes.

Combine confectioners sugar, aniseeds and lemon juice; beat

until smooth and of spreading consistency. Spread on warm
rolls. Makes 2 dozen frosted rolls.

SWIRLED HERBED BREAD

Serve with a main dish salad—sage and parsley add the flavor

1 (13¾ oz.) pkg. hot roll mix	1 tsp. pepper
3 tblsp. melted butter or	½ tsp. parsley flakes
regular margarine	¼ tsp. rubbed sage
⅓ c. grated Parmesan cheese	1 tblsp. melted butter
1 tsp. onion powder	

Prepare roll mix according to package directions. Let rise in
warm place until doubled. Punch down. Roll dough on lightly
floured board into an 18×9″ rectangle. Brush with 3 tblsp.
melted butter.

Mix cheese, onion powder, pepper, parsley and sage; sprinkle
over dough. Roll as for jelly roll, starting from shorter side; seal
seam. Place in greased 9×5×3″ loaf pan. Brush top with 1
tblsp. melted butter; cover and let rise until doubled, about 25
minutes.

Bake in moderate oven (375°) 35 to 45 minutes. Remove
from pan and cool on rack. Makes 1 loaf.

ST. LUCIA'S CARDAMOM ROLLS

Make ahead and freeze. Great for any special breakfast

2 pkgs. active dry yeast	¾ c. scalded milk
½ c. warm water (110 to 115°)	1 egg
⅓ c. sugar	3½ c. sifted flour (about)
2 tsp. salt	Raisins
1 tsp. ground cardamom	1 egg white
½ c. butter	

Soften yeast in warm water.

Place sugar, salt, cardamom and butter in large bowl. Add
hot milk; mix well and cool to lukewarm. Stir in yeast, egg and

2 c. flour. Beat until batter falls in sheets from a spoon. Add enough remaining flour to make a soft dough that leaves the sides of the bowl. Knead dough on lightly floured board until smooth and satiny, about 5 minutes. Place in greased bowl; turn dough over to grease top. Cover and let rise in warm place until doubled, about 1½ hours.

Punch down dough, and shape into a ball. Cover and let rest 10 minutes. Divide dough in 36 pieces. Roll each piece 12" long and ½" thick. Coil each end; put two rolls together back to back. Place a raisin in center of each coil. Place rolls on greased baking sheet; brush with egg white that has been beaten only until foamy. Cover and let rise in warm place until doubled, about 40 minutes.

Bake in hot oven (400°) 10 to 12 minutes. Makes 18 rolls.

NOTE: If desired, form the 12" rolls of dough in the shape of an "S," coiling or curling the ends. Stick a raisin in each coil.

ANISE TWISTS

Surprise your family with these anise-flavored rolls on Sunday

2 pkgs. active dry yeast	1½ tsp. ground aniseeds
½ c. warm water (110 to 115°)	2 eggs
¾ c. milk	5 c. sifted flour
½ c. sugar	1 egg, beaten
½ c. soft butter	⅓ c. sugar
1 tsp. salt	½ tsp. ground aniseeds

Sprinkle yeast on warm water; stir to dissolve.

Scald milk; pour into large bowl. Add ½ c. sugar, butter, salt and 1½ tsp. ground aniseeds. Stir until butter is melted. Let cool to lukewarm.

Beat 2 eggs into lukewarm milk mixture. Stir in yeast. Gradually add flour, first with wooden spoon, then with hand to make a dough that leaves sides of bowl.

Turn dough onto floured board. Cover and let rest 10 minutes. Knead until smooth and elastic. Place in lightly greased bowl; turn over to grease top. Cover and let rise in warm place until doubled, about 1 hour. Punch down, pull edges into center and turn over. Let rise 15 minutes.

On lightly floured board roll out dough to a 16×10½" rectangle. Cut in 3 lengthwise strips, then cut each strip crosswise in 1" pieces. Twist each strip several times and place on greased baking sheet. Let rise until almost doubled, 30 to 40 minutes. Immediately before baking, brush with beaten egg.

Combine ⅓ c. sugar and ½ tsp. ground aniseeds; sprinkle over tops of twists. Bake in moderate oven (375°) 12 minutes, or until golden brown. Remove to racks. Makes 4 dozen.

FROSTED RUM ROLLS

Attractive, easy-to-make rolls with pronounced rum flavor

1 (8 oz.) pkg. crescent refrigerated dinner rolls

1 c. confectioners sugar
3 tblsp. rum or rum flavoring
1 tblsp. sesame seeds

Separate rolls.

Mix sugar and rum. Spread over each roll triangle, reserving some for top. Starting at the wide end of triangle, roll up and curve into a crescent. Place on baking sheet.

Bake in moderate oven (375°) 12 minutes, or until golden brown. While still hot, spread each crescent with reserved sugar mixture. Sprinkle with sesame seeds. Makes 8 rolls.

NOTE: If you like a less pronounced rum flavor, use 1½ tblsp. water and 1½ tblsp. rum or rum flavoring instead of the 3 tblsp. called for in recipe.

CARAWAY/NUT ROLLS

Dress up simple refrigerated rolls and make them different

⅓ c. chopped pecans
1 tsp. caraway seeds

1 (8.6 oz.) can refrigerated snowflake dinner rolls

Combine pecans and caraway seeds in small bowl.

Separate roll dough into 18 pieces; put 2 pieces together for each roll. Coat with nut mixture. Stand rolls on edge in greased muffin-pan cups.

Bake in moderate oven (375°) 12 to 14 minutes, or until golden brown. Serve hot. Makes 9 rolls.

SAGEBRUSH MUFFINS

These muffins get their name from the pungent herb, sage

2 c. all-purpose buttermilk biscuit mix	1 egg
⅔ c. milk	½ tsp. rubbed sage

Combine biscuit mix, milk, egg and sage; mix just enough to moisten dry ingredients. Spoon batter into greased muffin-pan cups, filling half full.

Bake in very hot oven (450°) 12 to 15 minutes, or until brown and tops spring back when touched. Makes 12 muffins.

FENNEL SEED MUFFINS

If you've never tried fennel, you're in for a flavor surprise

2 c. sifted flour	¼ c. melted butter or regular margarine
¼ c. sugar	
1 tblsp. baking powder	1 egg
½ tsp. salt	1 c. milk
2 tblsp. fennel seeds	

Sift together flour, sugar, baking powder and salt. Blend in fennel seeds. Add butter, egg and milk. Stir just until all ingredients are blended. Fill medium-size muffin-pan cups two thirds full.

Bake in hot oven (400°) 20 to 25 minutes. Makes 12 muffins.

SAGE/BACON CORN MUFFINS

These hearty muffins are good accompaniments for any luncheon

1 (12 oz.) pkg. corn muffin mix	⅔ c. milk
¼ tsp. ground sage	½ c. crumbled crisp-cooked
1 egg	bacon

In large bowl combine corn muffin mix and sage. Make muffins according to package directions, adding the egg and milk. Fold in bacon. Turn into greased medium-size muffin-pan cups.

Bake in hot oven (400°) 20 to 25 minutes, or until done. Serve hot. Makes 12 muffins.

CINNAMON APPLESAUCE MUFFINS

Your family will gladly come to breakfast when they smell these

2 c. sifted flour	¼ c. shortening, melted
¼ c. sugar	½ c. chopped dates or raisins
3 tsp. baking powder	¼ tsp. ground aniseeds
½ tsp. salt	2 tblsp. sugar
½ tsp. ground cinnamon	½ tsp. ground cinnamon
2 eggs, beaten	1 tblsp. melted butter or
1 c. milk	regular margarine
½ c. applesauce	

Sift together flour, ¼ c. sugar, baking powder, salt and ½ tsp. cinnamon into mixing bowl.

Combine eggs, milk and applesauce; stir into sifted dry ingredients, using 14 strokes. Then stir in shortening, dates and aniseeds, using 8 to 10 strokes. Fill well-greased muffin-pan cups two thirds full.

Bake in hot oven (400°) 20 to 25 minutes, or until done. Remove from pan.

Meanwhile, combine 2 tblsp. sugar and ½ tsp. cinnamon. While still hot, dip muffin tops in melted butter, then in sugar-cinnamon mixture. Serve hot. Makes 15 muffins.

Quick and Easy Casseroles

Casserole dishes are ideal when you're having guests for dinner (who don't always arrive on time), or when some of your own family may be late. Most casseroles wait very nicely in a low oven, remaining hot without drying out. It's an advantage, too, to be able to assemble them hours before serving time, or even the day or evening before you entertain.

Meats, fish, eggs, poultry, cheese, macaroni, rice and noodles are all casserole ingredients making the variety of herbs that are good in casserole cookery almost unlimited. As a starter, try thyme and savory with meats, tarragon with seafoods, basil and parsley or dill with cheeses, Salad Herbs or the Fines Herbes blend with eggs. Herbs may be dried or fresh or you may use herb wine vinegars, or other of the herb blends (see Index for recipes). Chives and parsley are safe bets for any casserole and they can be used generously.

Canned soups such as mushroom, tomato, celery, asparagus and onion all have their proper companions. As substitutes for white sauces, gravies or other liquids, they're a flavorful shortcut. Beef or pork casseroles perk up with tomato soup, chicken and fish casseroles welcome mushroom soup, and the milder dishes are improved with consommé or beef broth.

A small amount of wine—sherry, sauterne, burgundy, Rhine, or rose—will add new flavor to your own old familiar recipes. One teaspoon per serving, added in place of other liquid, is a good general proportion.

Biscuit or pastry crusts dress up a casserole, and these are easy with the prepared mixes. Add a sprinkling of herbs to the top crust if you haven't used them in the mixture underneath.

CHILI BEEF CASSEROLE

Combination of herbs and spice blended with beef, rice and kidney beans results in a casserole with chili con carne flavor

1 lb. top round steak, cut in
   1″ cubes
1 c. finely chopped onion
2 tsp. chili powder
¼ tsp. dried orégano leaves,
   finely crumbled
1 tsp. garlic salt
2 tblsp. butter or regular
   margarine

⅔ c. raw regular rice
1 (15½ oz.) can red kidney
   beans
1 (1 lb.) can tomatoes
1 (10½ oz.) can condensed
   beef consommé

Combine meat, onion, chili powder, orégano and garlic salt. Brown in butter in skillet. Combine with rice, kidney beans, tomatoes and consommé; turn into 2-qt. casserole.

Cover and bake in moderate oven (350°) 1 hour and 15 minutes, or until meat is tender. Makes 6 servings.

SUMATRA MEAT PIE

Addition of Savory Meat Blend lifts dish out of the ordinary

2 tblsp. butter or regular
   margarine
1 lb. lean beef chuck, cut in
   1″ cubes
4 medium potatoes, pared and
   cubed
4 medium carrots, pared and
   cubed

4 medium onions, cubed
2 tblsp. cornstarch
1 c. water
1 tsp. Savory Meat Blend (see
   Index)
Pastry for 1-crust pie

Melt butter in 10″ skillet; add beef cubes and brown well. Add potatoes, carrots and onions; cook until onions are soft.

Blend cornstarch with water until smooth. Stir in Savory

Meat Blend. Add to skillet and cook, stirring until mixture thickens.

Roll out pastry slightly larger than top of skillet. (If your skillet cannot go into oven, transfer meat mixture to 2-qt. casserole.) Cut in strips 1" wide. Place strips about 1" apart over meat mixture, crisscrossing to make a lattice top. Press firmly to seal strips to rim.

Bake in hot oven (400°) 35 minutes, or until crust is golden brown and meat mixture is bubbling. Makes 4 to 6 servings.

BEEF AND MUSHROOM CASSEROLE

The secret to the seasoning in this meat-and-vegetable dish is the addition of Herb Salt—it does something special to beef

1 lb. top round steak
2 tblsp. butter or regular margarine
8 small whole onions, peeled
1 (6 oz.) can button mushrooms, drained
1 (1 lb.) can whole potatoes, drained

1 (10½ oz.) can condensed tomato soup
1 tsp. Worcestershire sauce
1 tsp. Herb Salt (see Index)
1 c. quick-cooking rice

Cut steak in 2×1" strips.

Melt butter in electric skillet; add steak and onions. Sauté until steak is brown. Add mushrooms, potatoes, tomato soup, Worcestershire sauce and Herb Salt. Stir to mix. Cover and simmer about 15 minutes.

Meanwhile, prepare rice according to package directions. Line 2-qt. casserole with rice. Pour steak mixture over rice.

Bake in slow oven (300°) 15 minutes. Makes 6 servings.

CHUM LUM RICE CASSEROLE

Marjoram and veal combined in a quick dish that's hard to beat

2 tblsp. butter or regular
  margarine
1 lb. veal, cut in small cubes
1 medium green pepper, finely
  chopped
1 c. quick-cooking rice

1 (10½ oz.) can condensed
  beef consommé
1 tsp. salt
¼ tsp. pepper
½ tsp. dried marjoram leaves,
  finely crumbled

Melt butter in large skillet; add veal cubes and brown well. Add green pepper and rice; stir to mix. Add consommé, salt, pepper and marjoram, stirring well.

Cover and cook over low heat 30 minutes, or until veal is tender. Makes 4 to 6 servings.

VEAL/HERB CASSEROLE

Thyme, basil and sherry-seasoned rice contribute the excellent flavor to this colorful main dish

2 tblsp. butter or regular
  margarine
1 lb. veal, cut in 1″ cubes
¼ tsp. dried basil leaves,
  finely crumbled
¼ tsp. dried thyme leaves,
  finely crumbled
1 tsp. paprika

1 c. coarsely chopped celery
1 c. finely chopped onion
1 (1 lb.) can tomatoes
2 beef bouillon cubes
¾ c. boiling water
1¼ c. dry sherry
1 c. raw regular rice

Melt butter in large skillet; add veal cubes, basil, thyme and paprika. Cook over medium-high heat until meat is well browned on all sides. Add celery, onion and tomatoes. Cover and simmer 5 minutes.

Meanwhile, dissolve bouillon cubes in boiling water.

Combine all ingredients in 2-qt. casserole. Cover and bake in moderate oven (350°) 45 minutes. Makes about 6 servings.

PORK CHOPS EN CASSEROLE

This easy-to-make casserole is perfect for company

6 loin pork chops, ¾" thick
Salt
2 tblsp. butter or regular margarine
6 large potatoes, pared and sliced
3 large onions, sliced
3 tblsp. cornstarch

¾ c. cooking sherry
1½ c. tomato juice
¾ tsp. dried rosemary leaves, crumbled
¼ tsp. salt
¼ tsp. pepper
½ c. grated Parmesan cheese

Season pork chops with salt. Brown pork chops in melted butter on both sides in large skillet. Remove from skillet as they brown.

Place potato slices in 4-qt. casserole or baking dish. Top with onion slices, then pork chops.

Combine cornstarch, sherry, tomato juice, rosemary, ¼ tsp. salt and pepper; stir until smooth. Pour over casserole mixture.

Cover and bake in hot oven (400°) 45 minutes. Remove from oven. Sprinkle with Parmesan cheese. Continue baking, uncovered, 30 minutes or until pork chops and vegetables are tender. Makes 6 servings.

PORK CHOP/LIMA BEAN CASSEROLE

A luscious, hearty main dish that is certain to please your family

1½ c. dried baby lima beans
4 c. water
3 tsp. salt
6 pork chops
1 tsp. salt
2 tblsp. flour
2 tblsp. salad oil

⅓ c. ketchup
2 tblsp. brown sugar
½ c. finely chopped onion
½ tsp. dry mustard
¼ tsp. pepper
¼ tsp. garlic powder
1 bay leaf

Soak lima beans overnight in water. Next morning, add 3 tsp. salt, and bring to a boil. Reduce heat; cover and simmer 45 minutes, or until beans are almost tender. Drain, saving liquid (you'll need 1½ c.). Place beans in 11×7×1½" baking dish.

Season pork chops on both sides with 1 tsp. salt, then flour. Brown on both sides in hot oil. Place pork chops over beans in baking dish.

Combine 1½ c. bean liquid, ketchup, brown sugar, onion, dry mustard, pepper, garlic powder and bay leaf in skillet; bring to a boil. Scrape pan. Pour over beans and pork chops.

Cover with foil and bake in slow oven (325°) 1 hour, or until pork chops are tender. Remove foil and bake 30 minutes more. Remove bay leaf. Makes 6 servings.

PORK AND MACARONI CASSEROLE

A flavorful dish accented with basil; trim with parsley

2 tblsp. butter or regular margarine	1 (10½ oz.) can condensed cream of mushroom soup
1 lb. pork, cut in 1" cubes	1 tsp. salt
2 c. cooked elbow macaroni	½ tsp. dried basil leaves, finely crumbled
1 c. finely chopped onion	
1 c. tomato juice	¼ tsp. pepper

Melt butter in 10" skillet; add pork cubes and fry over medium heat until brown on all sides.

Add macaroni, onion, tomato juice, soup, salt, basil and pepper. Mix lightly and pour into 2-qt. casserole.

Bake in slow oven (300°) 20 minutes. Makes 6 servings.

PIERRE'S CASSEROLE

Another recipe in which Herb Mustard lends its flavorful touch, this time with the addition of tarragon leaves

1 c. canned sliced mushrooms	2 (10½ oz.) cans condensed
2 c. chopped cooked ham	chicken broth
⅓ c. sliced pimiento-stuffed	2 tblsp. Herb Mustard (see
olives	Index)
4 medium potatoes, cooked,	¼ tsp. pepper
pared and cubed	½ tsp. dried tarragon leaves,
2 hard-cooked eggs, finely	finely crumbled
chopped	

Combine all ingredients in large bowl and mix well. Turn into 2-qt. casserole.

Cover and bake in moderate oven (350°) 50 minutes. Makes 6 servings.

BAVARIAN SUPPER CASSEROLE

Sage and caraway add an unusual flavor combination to this dish

2 tblsp. instant minced onion	⅛ tsp. pepper
2 tblsp. water	⅛ tsp. salt
3 tblsp. butter or regular	1 medium head cabbage,
margarine	shredded
1 tsp. ground sage	1½ c. slivered cooked ham
1½ tsp. caraway seeds	

Combine instant minced onion with water and allow to stand 10 minutes to soften.

Melt butter in large heavy skillet. Add sage, caraway seeds, pepper, salt and onion; sauté 2 minutes. Stir in cabbage.

Cover and cook 10 to 15 minutes, or until cabbage is tender-crisp, stirring once. Toss in ham and cook until ham is heated. Serve immediately. Makes 6 servings.

HAM AND RICE BAKE

A quick supper dish that is certain to please the whole family

¼ c. butter or regular margarine	1 c. canned tomatoes
¼ c. minced onion	½ tsp. salt
2 c. chopped baked ham	½ tsp. parsley flakes
1 c. long-grain parboiled rice	¼ tsp. dried thyme leaves,
3 c. chicken broth	finely crumbled

Melt butter in skillet; add onion and ham, and cook 10 minutes. Add rice, chicken broth, tomatoes, salt, parsley and thyme; simmer until rice has absorbed most of the liquid, about 25 minutes. Pour into well-greased 2-qt. casserole.

Cover and bake in moderate oven (350°) about 30 minutes. Makes 4 servings.

CHICKEN/SPAGHETTI CASSEROLE

Tarragon teams well with chicken in this delicious budget dish

1 (8 oz.) pkg. thin spaghetti	1 tsp. salt
½ c. butter or regular margarine	½ tsp. dried tarragon leaves,
2 c. cubed cooked chicken	crumbled
1 (4 oz.) can sliced mushrooms,	½ c. chopped celery
drained	½ c. Parmesan cheese
1 c. milk	

Cook spaghetti according to package directions; drain, rinse and place in a bowl. Add butter and mix gently until butter is melted. Add chicken, mushrooms, milk, salt, tarragon and celery. Spoon into 2-qt. casserole.

Cover and bake in moderate oven (350°) about 40 minutes. Uncover and sprinkle with cheese; bake 5 more minutes. Makes 6 servings.

ZUCCHINI/SPAGHETTI CASSEROLE

A meatless main dish that can be easily doubled for a crowd

1 (8 oz.) pkg. spaghetti
½ c. butter
2 zucchini, about 6" long
1 c. coarsely diced peeled
　fresh tomatoes
½ c. chopped onion
1 tsp. salt
½ tsp. dried basil leaves, finely
　crumbled
½ c. Parmesan cheese

Cook spaghetti according to package directions; drain, rinse and place in large bowl. Mix gently with butter until butter is melted.

Wash and cut unpeeled zucchini into bite-size cubes (you'll have about 3 c.).

Add zucchini and tomatoes to spaghetti; then add onion, salt and basil, mixing gently. Place a layer of spaghetti mixture in 2-qt. casserole; sprinkle lightly with cheese. Repeat layers of spaghetti mixture and cheese until all is used.

Bake in moderate oven (350°) 45 minutes to 1 hour, or until zucchini is tender. Makes 4 to 6 servings.

Egg and Cheese Dishes

Egg and cheese dishes are naturally mild and respond beautifully to a union with herb seasonings. Basil, chives and parsley are good with eggs prepared any style. These three herbs blend equally well with all types of cheese dishes. Marjoram, savory, tarragon and thyme are also good with egg and cheese concoctions, but they're stronger-flavored and should be used in smaller quantities.

If a recipe calls for separated egg yolks and whites, do the separating as soon as you take the eggs from the refrigerator, for cold egg yolks are less likely to break.

For hard-cooked eggs, start the cooking in cold water, and the shells will be less likely to crack. To keep the yolks nicely in the center of the whites when hard-cooking them, stir the water gently as it begins to simmer. As soon as the eggs are cooked, plunge them into cold water and gently crack each shell in one place, preferably the narrow top of the egg. Then the shells will peel off more easily.

To make good use of leftover raw egg yolks, drop them in simmering, salted water and cook for about 5 minutes, then chill and grate or mince. Mix grated cheese with the grated egg yolk, adding ¼ teaspoon of Salad Herbs. Sprinkle as a topping on any clear, hot soup. Grated cheese mixed with basil makes a yummy sauce for any tomato dish—even plain stewed tomatoes.

Anything served "aux fines herbes" means "with herbs chopped very fine," and the Fines Herbes blend is ideal for mixing with egg and cheese dishes. The Herb Salt, too, goes in with no worry about the right amount to use—because if you salt to your normal taste, you'll get the herbs as a bonus. (See Index for recipes.)

Do try the recipes in this section; both cheese and eggs are high in protein and good for you.

CREAMED EGGS ON TOAST

The perfect choice for a quick lunch or a main dish for brunch

3 tblsp. butter	6 hard-cooked eggs, sliced
3 tblsp. flour	¾ tsp. salt
2 c. milk	½ tsp. dried marjoram leaves
1 tblsp. instant minced onion	$\frac{1}{16}$ tsp. pepper
½ c. shredded sharp process cheese	Toast
	Paprika

Melt butter in saucepan. Blend in flour until smooth. Add milk and instant minced onion; mix well. Stir and cook over medium heat until mixture thickens.

Add cheese, eggs, salt, marjoram and pepper; heat to melt cheese. Serve over toast; sprinkle top with paprika. Makes 6 servings.

MADRAS CURRIED EGGS

Meatless, yet so nutritious. Try it for next Sunday's supper

3 tblsp. butter or regular margarine	1 c. milk
3 tblsp. minced onion	¼ tsp. ground ginger
¼ c. flour	¼ tsp. garlic powder
1 tblsp. curry powder	8 hard-cooked eggs
1¼ c. chicken broth	2½ c. cooked rice
	1 tblsp. minced fresh parsley

Melt butter in large skillet. Add onion and sauté 3 minutes. Blend in flour; cook 2 minutes longer. Stir in curry powder, chicken broth, milk, ginger and garlic powder. Cook, stirring constantly, until mixture thickens.

Cut eggs in lengthwise halves; add to sauce just to heat. Serve over hot rice. Garnish with parsley. Makes 8 servings.

TARRAGON MUSHROOM SCRAMBLE

Serve with glasses of orange juice and hot, buttered biscuits

½ lb. fresh mushrooms, sliced
3 tblsp. butter or regular
  margarine
1 tsp. dried tarragon leaves,
  crumbled

8 eggs, beaten
½ tsp. onion powder
½ tsp. salt
1/16 tsp. pepper

Add mushrooms to melted butter in large skillet. Add tarragon and sauté over medium-high heat 4 to 5 minutes, stirring occasionally.

Combine eggs with onion powder, salt and pepper; mix well. Pour over mushrooms in skillet. Cook, stirring gently, 1 to 2 minutes, or until eggs are set. Makes 6 servings.

NOTE: You can use 1 (6 to 8 oz.) can sliced mushrooms instead of fresh ones. Drain and wipe mushrooms dry with paper toweling before adding to butter in skillet.

SHRIMP OMELET SUPREME

Eggs combined with tarragon and filled with a mixture of shrimp, mushrooms, bean sprouts and water chestnuts make this omelet special

6 eggs
2 tsp. soy sauce
¼ tsp. dried tarragon leaves,
  crumbled
1 (4½ oz.) can medium shrimp,
  drained and rinsed

1 (4 oz.) can sliced mushrooms,
  drained
½ c. bean sprouts, drained
½ c. water chestnuts, sliced
1 tblsp. butter
2 tblsp. butter

Combine eggs, soy sauce and tarragon; beat well. Add shrimp, mushrooms, bean sprouts and water chestnuts to 1 tblsp. melted butter in 10″ skillet. Heat mixture, stirring occasionally.

Melt 2 tblsp. butter in 10″ omelet pan or heavy skillet.

When butter is hot, add egg mixture. Cook slowly over low heat. As egg mixture starts to set around edges, gently pull it toward center, tilting pan so that uncooked egg will run to edges. When all of mixture seems set, spoon the shrimp/vegetable filling over half of omelet; fold other half of omelet over filling and brown slightly. Serve immediately. Makes 3 or 4 servings.

SHARP CHEESE OMELET

This tasty omelet is another recipe seasoned with Herb Salt

2 tblsp. butter or regular margarine	½ c. milk
	1 tsp. Herb Salt (see Index)
6 eggs, very well beaten	1 c. grated sharp process cheese

Melt butter in 10″ omelet pan or heavy skillet.

Using a fork, blend eggs with milk and Herb Salt, mixing lightly. When butter is hot, pour egg mixture into skillet. Cook slowly over low heat. As mixture starts to set around edges, gently pull it toward center, tilting pan so that uncooked egg will run to edges. When all of egg mixture seems set, sprinkle cheese over half of omelet; fold other half over cheese. Serve immediately. Makes about 4 servings.

MIDNIGHT MUSHROOM OMELET

A high-protein dish that is so easy on your food budget

1 (4 oz.) can sliced mushrooms, drained	½ c. milk
	¼ c. chili sauce
2 tsp. chopped onion	1 tsp. salt
2 tblsp. butter or regular margarine	½ tsp. dried basil leaves, finely crumbled
1 tsp. minced fresh parsley	¼ lb. sharp process cheese, grated (1 c.)
1 tsp. lemon juice	
6 eggs, very well beaten	

Sauté mushrooms and onion in melted butter in 10″ omelet pan or heavy skillet. Add parsley and lemon juice; stir well. Remove from skillet and set aside.

Mix together eggs, milk, chili sauce, salt and basil until well blended. Pour into skillet and cook slowly over low heat. As egg mixture starts to set around edges, gently pull it toward center, tilting pan so that uncooked egg will run to edges. When all of mixture seems set, sprinkle with cheese. Spoon mushroom mixture over half of omelet; fold other half of omelet over filling. Serve immediately. Makes 6 servings.

TARRAGON DEVILED EGGS

Make these for your next party—your guests will love them

6 hard-cooked eggs
¼ tsp. dried tarragon leaves, crumbled
¼ tsp. dry mustard
1 tsp. warm water
¼ c. mayonnaise
½ tsp. onion salt
½ tsp. lemon juice
Paprika

Cut eggs in lengthwise halves. Remove yolks; put through sieve, or mash with a fork in small bowl.

Mix tarragon and dry mustard with warm water. Let stand 10 minutes.

Blend egg yolks with tarragon-mustard mixture, mayonnaise, onion salt and lemon juice. Spoon into egg white halves; garnish with paprika. Chill 1 hour before serving. Makes 12 egg halves.

DEVILED EGGS AUX FINES HERBES

Add a gourmet touch to your picnic basket by including these herb-seasoned eggs—they'll disappear in a hurry

6 hard-cooked eggs
1 tblsp. Herb Mustard (see Index)
2 tblsp. mayonnaise
1 tblsp. Chive Wine Vinegar (see Index) or white wine vinegar

1 tsp. Fines Herbes (see Index)
1 tsp. salt
¼ tsp. pepper
1 tsp. paprika
6 pimiento-stuffed olives, cut in halves

Cut eggs in halves lengthwise. Remove yolks.

Mash yolks with a fork in a small bowl; mix with Herb Mustard, mayonnaise, Chive Wine Vinegar, Fines Herbes, salt and pepper. Heap into egg white halves; sprinkle with paprika and garnish each with an olive half. Chill until ready to serve. Makes 12 egg halves.

FOOLPROOF BASIL CHEESE SOUFFLÉ

A soufflé that is easy to make and is also a guaranteed success

1½ c. milk
2 (1½ oz.) pkgs. cheese sauce mix
¾ tsp. onion powder

1 tblsp. dried basil leaves, crumbled
6 eggs, separated
½ tsp. cream of tartar

Combine milk, cheese sauce mix, onion powder and basil in saucepan. Bring to a boil, stirring constantly. Lower heat and simmer 1 minute, stirring constantly.

Beat egg yolks lightly. Stir in a little of the hot cheese sauce, then stir egg yolks into sauce in pan; blend thoroughly. Cook over medium heat 1 minute, stirring constantly. Remove from heat and cool slightly.

Combine egg whites and cream of tartar in large mixing bowl; beat until stiff but not dry. Gently fold in cheese sauce.

Grease 2-qt. straight-side soufflé dish on the bottom and pour in cheese mixture. Place soufflé dish in pan of water.

Bake in slow oven (325°) 1 hour, or until firm. Makes 6 servings.

HERBED CHEESE RAREBIT

Also good served on toasted English muffins with slices of ham

1 (10½ oz.) can condensed tomato soup

½ c. milk

½ lb. sharp process cheese, grated

1 tsp. salt

½ tsp. Savory Meat Blend (see Index)

2 tblsp. Herb Mustard (see Index)

2 tblsp. cornstarch

½ c. milk

1 tblsp. butter or regular margarine

4 to 6 slices toast

4 to 6 crisp-cooked bacon slices

Pour soup into top of double boiler over hot water. Gradually add ½ c. milk and cook, stirring constantly, until hot and blended.

Stir in cheese. Add salt, Savory Meat Blend and Herb Mustard; stir until cheese begins to melt.

Mix cornstarch with remaining ½ c. milk; stir until smooth. Add to cheese mixture, stirring constantly. Cook until mixture thickens slightly. Blend in butter. Serve over toast and garnish with bacon slices. Makes 4 to 6 servings.

MACARONI AU GRATIN WITH HERBS

Complete the menu with coleslaw and golden corn bread sticks

1 (8 oz.) pkg. elbow macaroni

½ lb. sharp Cheddar cheese, grated

1 c. milk or light cream

2 tblsp. minced onion

2 tblsp. Herb Mustard (see Index)

1 tblsp. minced fresh parsley

½ tsp. Herb Salt (see Index)

Cook macaroni according to package directions 6 to 7 minutes. Drain.

Combine macaroni with cheese, milk, onion, Herb Mustard, parsley and Herb Salt; spoon into 2-qt. casserole.

Bake in moderate oven (350°) 30 minutes; remove from oven and stir macaroni. Return to oven and bake 15 minutes longer, or until brown and bubbly. Makes 4 servings.

Seafood Specialties

What herbs to use with fish and shellfish? Basil, chives, dill, garlic, marjoram, mint, orégano, parsley, rosemary, savory, tarragon and thyme—almost the whole array of herbs.

Herb Butter (see Index) is simply marvelous for broiled fish. Dot it generously over fish before broiling. Melt Herb Butter and serve it as a dipping sauce for lobster, crab and shrimp. Herb sauces with fish dress up your menus unbelievably.

Herb wine vinegars (see Index for recipes) are truly valuable in cooking fish; marinating fish with any of these will take away the fishy taste some people object to. Cod, haddock, herring or any of the flat fish will become light and delicate when marinated in an herb vinegar, as if Chef Papa Escoffier himself had done the cooking.

Remember not to overcook fish, for it quickly becomes dry and tough. Cook just long enough to develop flavor; fish is naturally tender.

Since fish is an extremely high-protein food, we should eat it often—and learn to cook it in more versatile ways. We're all inclined to get in a rut, thinking fish must be fried or broiled; but what we do to the fish before or while cooking makes a world of difference in the final dish.

The recipes which follow may help you to become a more venturesome cook with fish.

BAKED FISH WITH RICE STUFFING

A whole meal in a dish . . . just add a crisp salad and rolls

¼ c. celery flakes
1 tblsp. instant minced onion
¼ c. water
2 c. cooked rice
3 tblsp. melted butter or regular margarine
1 tblsp. parsley flakes

1 tsp. salt
½ tsp. dried thyme leaves
⅛ tsp. pepper
1 (4 lb.) fish (blue or bass), cleaned
Salad oil or melted butter

Combine celery flakes and instant minced onion with water; let stand 8 minutes to soften. Add rice, 3 tblsp. melted butter, parsley, salt, thyme and pepper; mix gently until blended. Spoon mixture into cavity of fish. Close cavity with skewers or wooden picks, and brush with salad oil. Place in greased shallow baking pan.

Bake in moderate oven (375°) 40 minutes, or until fish flakes easily with a fork. Makes 6 servings.

FILLET OF FLOUNDER SUPREME

So easy to prepare . . . a good choice when you are late

4 large flounder fillets
2 tblsp. mayonnaise
3 tblsp. melted butter or regular margarine
2 tblsp. capers

1 tsp. dried tarragon leaves, finely crumbled
½ tsp. salt
¼ tsp. pepper

Spread flounder fillets in buttered 13×9×2″ baking pan.

Combine mayonnaise, butter, capers, tarragon, salt and pepper. Stir until mixture is blended and smooth. Spread evenly over fish.

Bake in hot oven (400°) 10 minutes, then place under broiler 3 to 5 minutes, until bubbly on top. Makes 4 servings. Double recipe and bake 2 pans of flounder for 8 servings.

SAVORY BAKED FISH

Tarragon is delightful with fish . . . your family will like it

1½ lbs. haddock fillets	½ tsp. dry mustard
½ tsp. salt	2 tsp. water
1 tsp. instant minced onion	1 tsp. lemon juice
¼ tsp. dried tarragon leaves	½ c. mayonnaise
1/16 tsp. pepper	Paprika

Wipe fish with a damp cloth and place in greased 9″ square baking dish. Sprinkle with salt.

Combine instant minced onion, tarragon, pepper, dry mustard and water; let stand 10 minutes for flavors to blend. Add lemon juice and mayonnaise. Spread evenly over fish.

Bake in extremely hot oven (500°) 17 to 20 minutes, or until browned. Garnish with paprika. Makes 6 servings.

SHRIMP CREOLE

An old Southern favorite which is perfect for company or family

¼ c. olive oil or salad oil	1 tsp. salt
3 tblsp. flour	½ tsp. sugar
1 (1 lb. 12 oz.) can tomatoes	½ tsp. dried thyme leaves,
½ c. water	crumbled
¼ c. onion flakes	⅛ tsp. pepper
¼ c. sweet pepper flakes	⅛ tsp. ground red pepper
¼ c. celery flakes	1 lb. large shrimp, cooked and
1 tblsp. parsley flakes	cleaned
1 bay leaf	Cooked rice

Heat oil in large saucepan; stir in flour. Cook, stirring constantly, until flour is lightly browned. Add tomatoes and water. Bring to a boil. Add onion, sweet pepper, celery and parsley flakes. Cover and simmer over low heat 10 minutes.

Add bay leaf, salt, sugar, thyme, pepper and red pepper; continue cooking 10 minutes longer. Just before serving add shrimp.

Cook about 5 minutes, or until shrimp are heated. Remove bay leaf. Serve over cooked rice. Makes 6 servings.

SEA KABOBS

Try also with this combination: pineapple and green pepper

¼ c. salad oil	2 (8 oz.) frozen lobster tails,
3 tblsp. cider vinegar	cooked
1 tblsp. lemon juice	1 lb. large shrimp, cooked and
¾ tsp. garlic salt	cleaned
½ tsp. dried thyme leaves,	1 medium zucchini, cut in ½″
crushed	slices
½ tsp. onion salt	¾ lb. mushrooms
½ tsp. salt	Cherry tomatoes
¼ tsp. pepper	

Combine oil, vinegar, lemon juice, garlic salt, thyme, onion salt, salt and pepper in small saucepan. Heat to boiling. Set aside to cool.

Remove shells from lobster tails and cut meat into chunks. Place lobster pieces on skewers, alternating with shrimp, zucchini and mushrooms. Place cherry tomatoes on end of skewers.

Broil, basting with sauce, 3 minutes, or until shrimp are lightly browned. Makes 6 servings.

SCALLOPED SALMON

Serve with buttered broccoli spears and tangy cabbage salad

1 (7¾ oz.) can salmon	¼ tsp. dried marjoram leaves,
1 tblsp. lemon juice	crumbled
1¼ c. cracker crumbs	¼ tsp. onion powder
⅓ c. melted butter	1 c. milk, scalded
½ tsp. salt	Lemon slices
1 tsp. dry mustard	Fresh parsley
¼ tsp. pepper	

Drain salmon; flake and mix with lemon juice.

Combine cracker crumbs, butter, salt, dry mustard, pepper, marjoram and onion powder. Put half of crumbs in 9″ pie pan; spread salmon over crumbs. Pour milk over top, and sprinkle with remaining crumbs.

Bake in hot oven (400°) 20 to 25 minutes. Garnish with lemon slices and parsley. Makes 4 or 5 servings.

SAVORY TUNA LOAF

Garnish the platter with sprigs of parsley and carrot curls

3 (7 oz.) cans water-pack tuna	½ tsp. dried thyme leaves, crushed
1½ c. fine bread crumbs	
2 eggs	¼ tsp. pepper
2 tblsp. instant minced onion	¼ tsp. garlic powder
1 tblsp. parsley flakes	1 tblsp. lemon juice
1½ tsp. salt	⅔ c. milk

Drain tuna, saving liquid. Flake tuna into a bowl; add bread crumbs, eggs, instant minced onion, parsley, salt, thyme, pepper, garlic powder, lemon juice, milk and liquid from tuna. Mix lightly. Spoon into greased 8½ ×4½ ×2½″ loaf pan.

Bake in moderate oven (350°) 1 hour, or until browned. Turn out onto platter. Slice, and serve with your favorite mushroom sauce, if you like. Makes 6 servings.

SALMON LOAF PARISIENNE

A flavorful dill sauce makes this salmon loaf company fare

1 (1 lb.) can salmon, drained	2 tblsp. Tarragon Wine Vinegar (see Index) or red wine vinegar
1 (10½ oz.) can condensed cream of celery soup	
1 egg, well beaten	1 c. cooked regular rice
1 tblsp. minced fresh parsley	Dill Sauce (see Index)

Discard skin and bones from salmon, and flake. Combine salmon, soup, egg, parsley, vinegar and rice; mix thoroughly. Spoon into lightly greased 8½ ×4½ ×2½ " loaf pan.

Bake in moderate oven (350°) about 1 hour. Serve with Dill Sauce. Makes 6 servings.

SCALLOPED SCALLOPS

It's the peppery sauce, uniting wine and chives, that enhances tender scallops and potatoes in an easy-to-make main dish

1 lb. scallops
4 medium potatoes, pared and sliced
1 c. medium-dry sauterne
¼ c. fresh or frozen chopped chives
2 tblsp. butter or regular margarine
1 tsp. salt
½ tsp. pepper
2 tblsp. cornstarch
½ c. light cream

Place alternate layers of scallops and potato slices in 2-qt. casserole.

Pour sauterne into small saucepan; add chives, butter, salt and pepper.

Blend cornstarch with cream until smooth; add slowly to saucepan and cook over low heat, stirring constantly, until smooth. Pour over scallops and potatoes.

Bake in moderate oven (350°) 1¼ hours, or until potatoes are tender. Makes 6 servings.

Marvelous Meat Dishes

Herbs are more than just a seasoning—they're a whole philosophy of cookery in themselves. But don't overdo them; don't use so much of an herb that you're conscious of its presence in a dish. Too little is better than too much, as we've said before. You want just a hint of that aromatic flavor.

If you haven't yet discovered what herb wine vinegars can do for meats, you don't know what you're missing. The wine vinegars, especially when combined with herbs, add distinctive flavor. The longer the meat marinates, the better the flavor. Tough meat is tenderized in wine vinegar. Until you try it, you won't believe that the meat *does not* taste vinegarish when cooked. Please don't overlook the Herb Marinade (see Index).

After marinating, meat can be cooked in any manner—baked, broiled, roasted, fried or stewed. Marinate first, then follow one of these recipes.

You needn't be too concerned about the right herb with the right meat. All the tangy meat herbs are interchangeable. Sage is a natural in sausage, but it does wonders for roast beef, ham or roast pork, too. Thyme is perfect for beef and it blends well in an endless variety of casseroles. Basil is splendid for stews and meat-egg-cheese combinations. Marjoram is superb with lamb, veal and poultry. Savory is good with *any* meat dish. Rosemary is especially fine with beef, pork, poultry and game.

Use ¼ teaspoon of dried herbs or 1 teaspoon of fresh chopped herbs on meat to serve 4 people. You may find you like more, after you've gotten acquainted with herbs, but start out with this amount.

Do try using Herb Butter (see Index) to spread on meats before broiling. Try adding 2 tablespoons of any herb wine vinegar to hamburger or ground beef before making patties, meat loaf or any other ground beef recipe.

And don't forget to add herbs to gravy or sauces, if you haven't used them in the meat. Mix ¼ teaspoon of dried herbs with your thickening before adding to the liquids.

A special afterthought: Herbs make hash a chef's specialty.

STUFFED FLANK STEAK

An inexpensive cut of meat that is transformed into elegant fare with slow cooking and expert herb seasoning

6 tblsp. bacon drippings	¼ tsp. pepper
1½ c. soft bread cubes	3 slices crisp-cooked bacon,
1½ c. mashed potatoes	crumbled
3 tblsp. instant minced onion	¼ c. hot water
3 tsp. parsley flakes	1½ lbs. flank steak
¾ tsp. salt	¾ c. water
¾ tsp. poultry seasoning	

Combine bacon drippings, bread cubes, potatoes, instant minced onion, parsley, salt, poultry seasoning, pepper and bacon; mix well. Gradually add ¼ c. hot water.

Score steak lightly on both sides in 1½″ squares. Pound on both sides with a meat mallet or edge of heavy plate to break down fibers. Spread with stuffing to within ½″ of edge. Roll up jelly-roll fashion. Tie roll in 3 or 4 places with string and place seam side down on rack in 13×9×2″ baking pan. Add ¾ c. water.

Cover and bake in slow oven (325°) 1 hour and 15 minutes, or until meat is tender. To serve, cut in crosswise slices. Makes 6 servings.

HONG KONG STEAK

The Salad Herbs add much to this easy oriental-style beef dish

1 lb. round steak
2 tblsp. butter or regular
  margarine
1 (3 oz.) can button
  mushrooms, drained
1 (8½ oz.) can water chestnuts,
  drained and sliced

1 (6 oz.) can bamboo shoots
2 tblsp. soy sauce
¼ tsp. Salad Herbs (see Index)
1 (7 oz.) pkg. frozen pea pods

Cut steak in strips about 1" wide and 2" long. Melt butter in electric skillet set at 350° and brown steak on all sides.

Reduce heat to 250°. Add mushrooms, water chestnuts, bamboo shoots, soy sauce and Salad Herbs. Cover and cook over low heat (250°) about 25 minutes, or until steak is tender.

Add pea pods and cook just until thawed, heated and still crisp, about 5 minutes. Serve with additional soy sauce, if you like. Makes 4 servings. Double recipe for 8 servings.

FLORIDA SWISS STEAK

This unusual blend of flavors will surprise and delight you

2 lbs. top round steak, cut about
  1" thick
Instant meat tenderizer
2 tblsp. horseradish
2 tblsp. light cream

1 tsp. salt
¼ tsp. pepper
1 c. chopped onion
1 c. grapefruit juice
2 tblsp. flour

Sprinkle both sides of steak with meat tenderizer as label directs. Place in greased shallow baking pan.

Mix horseradish, light cream, salt and pepper, and spread on steak. Press onion over top.

Mix grapefruit juice with flour and cook, stirring, until mixture is slightly thickened. Pour gently over and around steak.

Cover and bake in moderate oven (350°) 1 hour. Uncover and bake 30 minutes longer, or until steak is tender. Makes 4 servings. Double recipe and bake in large shallow pans for 8 servings.

SWISS STEAK WITH HERBS

Steak is covered with an herb-seasoned tomato sauce that gives off a tantalizing aroma as it bakes

¼ c. flour
2 lbs. top round steak, cut
   1″ thick
2 tblsp. salad oil
2 large onions, thinly sliced
⅔ c. coarsely chopped celery
1 (1 lb.) can tomatoes
1 tblsp. soy sauce

2 tblsp. Herb Mustard (see
   Index)
1 tsp. Savory Meat Blend (see
   Index)
1 tsp. Worcestershire sauce
1 tsp. salt
½ tsp. pepper

Pound flour into both sides of steak with edge of heavy plate or meat mallet; brown on both sides in oil in large skillet. Place meat in 11×7×1½″ baking dish. Top with onion slices and celery.

Combine tomatoes, soy sauce, Herb Mustard, Savory Meat Blend, Worcestershire sauce, salt and pepper; pour over meat.

Cover with foil and bake in moderate oven (350°) 1 hour and 15 minutes, or until meat is tender and vegetables are well done. Makes 4 to 6 servings.

BEEF BARBARA

Chives, parsley and bamboo shoots lend distinction to round steak in this dish that will keep if dinner is late

1 lb. top round steak, cut in 1" cubes	1½ c. tomato juice
	1 tsp. salt
2 tblsp. salad oil	¼ tsp. pepper
¼ c. finely chopped fresh chives	½ tsp. parsley flakes
	1 (5 oz.) can bamboo shoots, drained
1 green pepper, finely chopped	

Brown steak cubes in salad oil. Divide pieces evenly among 4 individual casseroles.

Combine chives, green pepper, tomato juice, salt, pepper, parsley and bamboo shoots. Spoon evenly over meat in casseroles.

Cover and bake in moderate oven (350°) 1 hour and 15 minutes, or until steak is tender. Makes 4 servings. Double recipe for 8 servings.

NOTE: For individual meat pies, roll out pastry 1" larger than top of each casserole. Place over meat mixture; fold under and flute against inside edge of casserole. Cut steam vents in center. Bake as directed.

COUNTRY FRIED STEAK

Serve with fluffy mashed potatoes and parsley-buttered carrots

½ c. flour	1 tsp. salt
2 lbs. round steak, cut 1 to 1½" thick	1 tblsp. flour
	1 c. water
¼ c. salad oil	¼ tsp. salt
½ tsp. Savory Meat Blend (see Index)	1 tsp. instant minced onion

With meat mallet or edge of heavy plate, pound ½ c. flour well into steak on each side.

Heat oil in 10″ electric skillet set at 375°. Add steak and fry 15 minutes; turn, sprinkle with Savory Meat Blend and 1 tsp. salt and fry 10 minutes more for medium steak, longer if you prefer well-done meat. Remove steak to hot platter while you make gravy.

Brown 1 tblsp. flour in fat that remains in skillet. Add water, ¼ tsp. salt and instant minced onion. Cook over low heat, stirring constantly until thickened, scraping loose any brown flecks in skillet. Serve with steak. Makes 4 to 6 servings.

NOTE: If you like, sprinkle steak with seasoned instant meat tenderizer, following directions on label. Then cook as directed above.

ROAST STEAK AND VEGETABLES

To complete meal, pass a large plate of assorted relishes

1 lb. top round steak, cut 1″ thick	¼ c. flour
2 tblsp. salad oil	1 (1 lb.) can tomato wedges
2 tblsp. Herb Mustard (see Index)	3 medium potatoes, pared and quartered
¼ tsp. dried basil leaves, finely crumbled	3 carrots, pared and cut in ½″ pieces
¼ tsp. dried marjoram leaves, finely crumbled	1 c. frozen peas
¼ tsp. parsley flakes, finely crumbled	1 onion, sliced
	1 tsp. salt
	½ tsp. pepper

In 10″ skillet, brown meat quickly on each side in hot oil (just a minute or two per side). Place meat in 13×9×2″ pan.

Mix Herb Mustard, basil, marjoram, parsley and flour with tomatoes. Pour over steak. Arrange potatoes, carrots, peas and onion slices around steak. Sprinkle with salt and pepper.

Bake in moderate oven (350°) about 1 hour, or until vegetables are done. Makes 4 servings. Double recipe and bake in 2 pans for 8 servings.

STUFFED BEEF ROLLS

Sage and rosemary blend together well in this budget beef dish

2 tblsp. butter or regular
  margarine
1 medium onion, finely
  chopped
¼ tsp. rubbed sage
¼ tsp. dried rosemary leaves,
  finely crumbled

2 c. dry bread crumbs
1 to 2 tblsp. water
2 lbs. top round steak, cut
  ¼" thick
1 (10½ oz.) can condensed
  tomato soup
¼ c. water

Melt butter in skillet; add onion, sage and rosemary, and cook until onion is tender. Combine with bread crumbs and add just enough water (1 to 2 tblsp.) to hold mixture together.

Cut steak slices in 4" squares. Top each square with stuffing; roll and place seam side down in 11×7×1½" baking pan.

Combine soup and ¼ c. water; pour over meat in pan. Cover and bake in moderate oven (350°) 1 hour and 30 minutes, or until meat is tender. Makes 6 servings.

BEEF ROBERT

This yummy oven-baked stew is both hearty and nutritious

¼ c. flour
1 tsp. Savory Meat Blend (see
  Index)
1 tsp. salt
½ tsp. pepper
2 lbs. beef chuck, cut in 1½"
  cubes

2 tblsp. salad oil
2 (10¾ oz.) cans condensed
  golden mushroom soup
12 small potatoes, pared
6 small onions, peeled
6 carrots, pared and cut in
  ½" slices

Combine flour, Savory Meat Blend, salt and pepper. Place in plastic or paper bag; add meat cubes and toss to coat well.

Brown meat on all sides in oil in large skillet. Transfer meat to 2½-qt. casserole. Add soup.

Cover and bake in moderate oven (350°) 1 hour. Add vegetables and bake 30 minutes longer, or until meat and vegetables are tender. Makes 6 servings.

SALISBURY STEAKS

Rosemary and cream-style corn make these patties so unusual

1 lb. ground chuck
1 c. dry bread crumbs
1 (8¾ oz.) can cream-style corn
1 egg, slightly beaten
½ c. finely chopped onion
¼ tsp. dried rosemary leaves, finely crumbled

1 tsp. parsley flakes, finely crumbled
1 tsp. salt
1 (4 oz.) can sliced mushrooms, drained
¼ c. dry sherry
⅓ c. chopped pimiento-stuffed olives

Combine ground chuck, bread crumbs, corn, egg, onion, rosemary, parsley and salt; mix thoroughly. Shape into patties about 1″ thick and 3″ in diameter. Place in shallow baking pan.

Mix mushrooms with sherry, and pour over meat patties. Bake in moderate oven (350°) 25 to 30 minutes. Sprinkle top of patties with chopped olives. Makes 6 servings.

CARL'S GROUND BEEF IN GRAVY

A nourishing main dish that's easy to fix; Savory Meat Blend is the special seasoning. Serve it over mashed potatoes

2 tblsp. butter or regular margarine
1 lb. ground chuck
1 large onion, finely chopped
1 tsp. salt

½ tsp. Savory Meat Blend (see Index)
2 tblsp. flour
1½ c. milk

Melt butter in 9″ skillet; add meat, onion, salt and Savory Meat Blend. Place over medium heat, breaking meat into small pieces with a fork. Cook until meat turns color and onions are tender.

Stir in flour; cook and stir about 1 minute, or until flour is

well blended. Slowly add milk, stirring constantly. Cook over
low heat until sauce is smooth and thickened. Cover and simmer
about 10 minutes. Makes about 4 servings. Double recipe for 8
servings.

POULETTES

*Little beef patties wear a topping of Herb Mustard, peanut butter
and cheese, sprinkled with mixed herbs*

1 lb. ground beef
2 tblsp. Herb Mustard (see
　Index)
2 tblsp. peanut butter

¼ lb. sharp process cheese,
　sliced
1 tsp. Salad Herbs (see Index)
1 c. cooking sherry

Form beef into very small patties, about the size of a silver
dollar. Brown in skillet on both sides. Pour off any fat. (If beef
is extra lean, it may be necessary to add a little fat to skillet
before browning.) Place a dab of Herb Mustard on each patty,
then a dab of peanut butter. Top with a slice of cheese.

Sprinkle Salad Herbs over meat patties. Add sherry; cover
and simmer about 20 minutes. Makes 4 to 6 servings.

ROYAL MEAT LOAF

*A really different meat loaf—ground beef combined with deviled
ham and two special herb blends. You'll want to try it*

2 lbs. ground chuck
2 tblsp. chili sauce
2 eggs, slightly beaten
¼ c. milk
1 (4½ oz.) can deviled ham

2 tblsp. Herb Mustard (see
　Index)
1 c. fresh bread crumbs
1 tblsp. Savory Meat Blend
　(see Index)

Combine meat, chili sauce, eggs, milk, deviled ham, Herb
Mustard, bread crumbs and Savory Meat Blend; mix together
thoroughly. Pack into greased 9×5×3″ loaf pan.

Bake in moderate oven (350°) about 1 hour. Let stand 15
minutes before cutting. Makes 6 servings.

CASTILIAN SPAGHETTI

This sauce is superbly seasoned with herbs and mushrooms

2 lbs. ground beef
2 c. finely chopped onion
1 clove garlic, mashed
1 (1 lb.) can tomatoes
2 (6 oz.) cans tomato paste
½ tsp. dried orégano leaves, finely crumbled
½ tsp. dried basil leaves, finely crumbled

½ tsp. dried thyme leaves, finely crumbled
½ tsp. parsley flakes, finely crumbled
1 tsp. salt
½ tsp. pepper
½ c. sliced fresh mushrooms
Cooked spaghetti
Grated Parmesan cheese

Brown ground beef, onion and garlic in large saucepan, breaking up meat with a fork to separate.

Add tomatoes, tomato paste, orégano, basil, thyme, parsley, salt, pepper and mushrooms. Stir to mix well. Cover and simmer 1 hour, stirring occasionally.

Serve over cooked spaghetti. Pass Parmesan cheese to sprinkle over top. Makes 6 cups sauce, enough for about 6 servings.

MEAT LOAF PIZZA SUPREME

If your children are pizza lovers, they'll go for this meat loaf

1 lb. ground beef
1 egg, slightly beaten
1 tsp. salt
⅛ tsp. pepper
2 (8 oz.) cans tomato sauce
½ c. dry bread crumbs
2 tblsp. grated Parmesan cheese

2 tblsp. olive oil
4 tsp. dried basil leaves, crumbled
2 tsp. instant minced onion
¼ tsp. garlic powder
5 or 6 thin slices mozzarella cheese

Combine ground beef, egg, salt and pepper in mixing bowl. Mix well, but lightly. Pat into bottom and around sides of 9″ pie pan. Set aside.

Combine tomato sauce, bread crumbs, Parmesan cheese, oil,

basil, instant minced onion and garlic powder in mixing bowl; spoon into meat-lined pie pan.

Bake in moderate oven (375°) 30 minutes. Remove from oven and top with mozzarella cheese. Return to oven for 5 minutes, or until cheese is melted. Let rest 5 minutes before cutting pizza in pie-shaped wedges. Makes 6 servings.

HERBED MEATBALLS WITH MUSHROOM SAUCE

For a change of pace, try serving with mashed potatoes or rice

1 lb. ground lean beef	¼ tsp. dried marjoram leaves,
¼ lb. pork sausage	crumbled
¼ c. dry bread crumbs	1 egg, slightly beaten
1 tsp. salt	2 tblsp. shortening
2 tblsp. tomato paste	1 (8 oz.) pkg. noodles, cooked
¼ tsp. dried thyme leaves,	Mushroom Sauce (recipe
crumbled	follows)

Combine ground beef, pork sausage, bread crumbs, salt, tomato paste, thyme, marjoram and egg. Shape in 1½" balls.

Brown meatballs in hot shortening in skillet. Reduce heat to low and cook about 10 minutes, or until tender. Serve over cooked noodles with Mushroom Sauce. Makes 18 meatballs, about 6 servings.

Mushroom Sauce: Combine 1 (10½ oz.) can condensed cream of mushroom soup with ½ c. water, 1 tsp. paprika, ¼ tsp. ground thyme and ⅟₁₆ tsp. garlic powder. Mix well and heat thoroughly. Serve over Herbed Meatballs.

CONTINENTAL MEAT PIE

This hearty herbed casserole will make a hit with your family

2 tblsp. butter or regular
   margarine
1 lb. ground chuck
1 c. finely chopped onion
½ c. finely chopped celery
½ c. coarsely chopped green
   pepper
1 (10½ oz.) can condensed
   tomato soup
1 tsp. Worcestershire sauce
½ tsp. salt

⅛ tsp. pepper
2 c. all-purpose buttermilk
   biscuit mix
1 tsp. parsley flakes, finely
   crumbled
¼ tsp. dried thyme leaves, finely
   crumbled
¼ c. milk
¼ c. salad oil
Ripe olives

Melt 2 tblsp. butter in large skillet. Add meat, onion, celery and green pepper; cook until meat is done and vegetables slightly tender. Stir in tomato soup, Worcestershire sauce, salt and pepper. Pour into 2-qt. shallow casserole.

Combine biscuit mix, parsley and thyme; add milk and oil, and mix with a fork. Roll out slightly larger than top of casserole. Place dough over beef mixture and fold edges under. Flute against inside of casserole; cut vents.

Bake in hot oven (400°) about 20 minutes, or until crust is golden brown. Before serving, gently tuck ripe olives into slits in crust. Makes 4 to 6 servings.

MEATBALL PAPRIKASH

Just before serving, sprinkle meatballs with fresh parsley

¼ c. instant minced onion	2 tblsp. salad oil
¾ c. milk	2 tblsp. flour
2 lbs. ground lean beef	1½ c. water
1 clove garlic, minced	1 beef bouillon cube
¾ c. soft bread crumbs	2 tblsp. paprika
1 egg, beaten	¼ tsp. salt
2 tsp. salt	1 c. dairy sour cream
¼ tsp. pepper	Hot, cooked rice

In large bowl add instant minced onion to milk and let stand 10 minutes. Add beef, garlic, bread crumbs, egg, 2 tsp. salt and pepper; mix well. Shape mixture into 1½″ balls.

Heat oil in large skillet. Add meatballs, a few at a time, and brown on all sides. Remove from skillet and set aside.

Stir flour into skillet; brown slightly. Gradually add water, blending until smooth. Add bouillon cube, paprika and ¼ tsp. salt. Cook, stirring until thickened. Blend in sour cream. Return meatballs to sauce; heat but do not boil. Serve with rice. Makes 30 meatballs, about 8 servings.

SWEET AND SOUR MEATBALLS

The sweet and sour sauce accents the well-seasoned meatballs

1 lb. ground beef	Salad oil
½ lb. bulk pork sausage	1 (8 oz.) can sliced pineapple
1 egg, slightly beaten	3 tblsp. cornstarch
¼ c. cornstarch	1 tblsp. soy sauce
½ tsp. salt	3 tblsp. cider vinegar
¼ tsp. pepper	½ c. sugar
2 tblsp. minced onion	1 c. water
¼ tsp. dry mustard	1 green pepper, coarsely
½ tsp. dried savory leaves,	chopped
finely crumbled	Hot, cooked rice

Mix beef and pork sausage, and add egg. Add ¼ c. cornstarch, salt, pepper, onion, dry mustard and savory; blend well. Form into small balls. Brown meatballs in very small amount of oil in skillet. Set aside.

Drain pineapple, reserving juice. Add enough water to juice to make 1 c. Cut pineapple in small pieces.

Mix pineapple juice, 3 tblsp. cornstarch, soy sauce and vinegar; add to pan drippings. Cook, stirring constantly, to make a smooth sauce. Add sugar, water, green pepper and pineapple; continue to stir until mixture thickens. Add meatballs and heat through. Serve with rice. Makes 4 to 6 servings.

COUNTRY-STYLE SPARERIBS

Serve with zippy barbecue sauce and fluffy mashed potatoes

¾ c. flour	3 lbs. spareribs, cut in 2-rib
1 tsp. salt	pieces
½ tsp. ground sage	¼ c. shortening
¼ tsp. pepper	Boiling water

Combine flour with salt, sage and pepper in plastic or paper bag. Add spareribs and toss to coat well.

Brown spareribs on both sides in hot shortening in large skillet. Add enough boiling water to almost cover meat. Cover and simmer about 1 hour and 30 minutes, or until meat is tender. Makes 4 servings. Double recipe for 8 servings.

BARBECUED RIBS WITH HERBS

This has a tangy taste you'll like; give the credit to Herb Mustard, Herb Salt, sage and a vinegar seasoned with basil

3 lbs. spareribs	1 tsp. dried sage leaves, finely
¼ c. Herb Mustard (see Index)	crumbled
¼ c. chili sauce	¼ c. Basil Wine Vinegar (see
¼ c. lemon juice	Index) or red wine vinegar
2 tsp. Herb Salt (see Index)	

Cut spareribs into 2-rib pieces.

Combine Herb Mustard, chili sauce, lemon juice, Herb Salt, sage and vinegar; mix well.

Place ribs in large roasting pan. Pour sauce over ribs. Bake in slow oven (325°) about 1 hour, turning ribs occasionally to coat with sauce. Makes 4 to 6 servings.

SOUTHERN SPARERIBS WITH SAUERKRAUT

A perfect duo—Savory Meat Blend and ribs; add dill pickle and you have a truly delicious dish

6 medium potatoes, pared and cut in halves	1 tsp. salt
2 (1 lb. 12 oz.) cans sauerkraut	½ tsp. Savory Meat Blend (see Index)
1 large (6″) dill pickle	1½ c. water
2 lbs. spareribs	

Place potato halves in bottom of large electric skillet. Spread sauerkraut evenly over top so potatoes are covered.

Cut pickle in lengthwise quarters and place 1 quarter in each corner of skillet.

Cut ribs into 2-rib pieces; place over sauerkraut. Sprinkle salt and Savory Meat Blend over ribs. Pour water over all. Add more water during cooking to keep contents from becoming dry or burning.

Set skillet temperature at 300°; cover and cook about 1 hour and 30 minutes, until ribs and potatoes are tender. Makes 6 servings.

PEPPY PORK SAUSAGE

There's nothing like homemade pork sausage . . . so easy, too!

1 lb. ground lean pork	½ tsp. ground thyme
1 lb. ground pork fat	½ tsp. ground red pepper
2 tblsp. water	¼ tsp. pepper
1 tsp. salt	$\frac{1}{16}$ tsp. garlic powder
1 tblsp. ground sage	

Mix together pork and fat. Add water, salt, sage, thyme, red pepper, pepper and garlic powder; mix together. Put through food chopper or grinder, using fine blade. Store in refrigerator overnight for flavors to blend.

To cook, shape mixture into patties. Brown on both sides in hot skillet. Makes 6 servings.

INDIVIDUAL HAM LOAVES

A great way to use leftover smoked ham—and so delicious

1 lb. ground smoked ham
½ lb. ground pork
2 tblsp. Herb Mustard (see Index)

1 egg, slightly beaten
¼ c. dark brown sugar, firmly packed
½ c. dry bread crumbs

Combine ham, pork, Herb Mustard, egg, brown sugar and bread crumbs; mix thoroughly. Pack into 3″ muffin-pan cups so that tops are rounded above the level of pan.

Bake in moderate oven (350°) 35 minutes. Makes 8 loaves.

POT ROASTED FRESH HAM

The marjoram and sauterne help bring out the best in this ham

½ c. flour
1 tsp. salt
1 tsp. pepper
½ tsp. dried marjoram leaves, crumbled

1 (5 lb.) fresh ham
2 tblsp. salad oil
1 c. sauterne or Rhine wine
2 tblsp. flour
2 tblsp. water

Combine ½ c. flour, salt, pepper and marjoram; rub mixture into meat, coating well on all sides. Brown meat on all sides in hot oil in Dutch oven.

Pour wine over meat; cover and bake in slow oven (300°) about 3 hours, or until meat is well done. Remove roast from pan, keeping it warm while you make gravy.

Skim fat from liquid in pan. Let remaining liquid cook down slightly. Mix 2 tblsp. flour and water to make a smooth paste;

stir into liquid in pan. Cook over low heat, stirring constantly, until gravy thickens and is bubbly. Makes about 1 cup gravy. Serve with roast. Makes 8 servings.

DEEP-BROWN LAMB CHOPS

Plan a small dinner party with these chops as the main entrée

4 large loin lamb chops
2 tblsp. butter or regular
  margarine
1 tsp. Worcestershire sauce

½ tsp. dried marjoram leaves,
  finely crumbled
2 tblsp. soy sauce

Place lamb chops in shallow baking pan. Spread each with butter. Place under broiler just long enough to melt butter. Sprinkle lamb chops with Worcestershire sauce, marjoram and 1 tblsp. soy sauce.

Bake in hot oven (400°) 10 minutes; turn, sprinkle remaining 1 tblsp. soy sauce over chops and bake 10 minutes longer, or until chops are tender. Remove chops to platter.

Skim fat from liquid in pan; spoon remaining juices over chops. Makes 4 servings. Double recipe for 8 servings.

MARINATED LAMB ROAST

These well-chosen seasonings add a new dimension to lamb

2 c. beef stock
2 tblsp. lemon juice
1½ tsp. whole allspice
1 bay leaf, crumbled
1 tsp. salt
1 tsp. whole cloves

½ tsp. ground thyme
½ tsp. rosemary leaves
½ tsp. pepper
1 (5 lb.) boned and rolled leg
  of lamb

Pour beef stock into saucepan; add lemon juice, allspice, bay leaf, salt, cloves, thyme, rosemary and pepper. Heat to boiling.

Pour marinade over lamb; cool. Let marinate in refrigerator 24 hours, turning meat several times.

Place lamb on rack in shallow baking pan. Cover and bake in

slow oven (325°) 2 hours, or until meat is almost tender, basting several times with marinade. Remove cover and roast 1 hour and 30 minutes longer, or until brown. Makes 8 to 10 servings.

LUNCHEON MEAT/VEGETABLE PIE

A good hot lunch for a cold autumn day . . . just add a salad

2 tblsp. butter or regular margarine

2 tblsp. flour

1 (10½ oz.) can condensed tomato soup

1 (12 oz.) can luncheon meat, diced

1 tsp. instant minced onion

1 (1 lb.) can mixed vegetables, undrained

½ tsp. ground thyme

¼ tsp. salt

¼ tsp. pepper

⅛ tsp. garlic powder

1 (8 oz.) can refrigerated biscuits

Melt butter in saucepan; blend in flour until smooth. Add tomato soup and cook until thickened. Stir in meat, instant minced onion, mixed vegetables, thyme, salt, pepper and garlic powder. Turn into 10×6×1½" baking pan. Top with biscuits.

Bake in hot oven (425°) 15 to 20 minutes. Serve immediately. Makes 6 servings.

Choice Chicken Dishes and Stuffings

What herbs do for poultry and game is sheer kitchen poetry. In these dishes, you can use a much more generous hand with herbs, especially when you prepare poultry and poultry stuffing. For chicken and turkey, 1 teaspoon of herbs per pound of bird is a good rule of thumb.

Here again, don't forget what herb wine vinegars can do. Try marinating poultry and especially game in the vinegars. You may also baste the meat once or twice with a bit of vinegar while it roasts. The wild taste of venison, duck and other game can be tastefully overcome by using herbs and herb vinegars.

For chicken dishes, tarragon is the best herb, but marjoram runs a close second. Turkey is splendid with basil, thyme, savory and sage. Thyme, tarragon and garlic improve the flavor of wild ducks and geese.

If you're fortunate enough to be able to serve pheasants or partridge, you'll find that rosemary or tarragon blends well with their natural flavors, enhancing but not disguising them.

Stuffings for any kind of poultry or game absolutely require the addition of one or more herbs.

TARRAGON CHICKEN WITH SOUR CREAM

Garnish the serving platter with fluffy parsley-buttered rice

1½ tsp. salt
1 (3 lb.) broiler-fryer, cut up
¼ c. butter or regular margarine
2 tblsp. flour
2 c. hot chicken broth
2 tblsp. instant minced onion

1 tsp. dried tarragon leaves, crumbled
¼ tsp. white pepper
¼ tsp. garlic powder
¾ c. dairy sour cream

Rub salt into chicken. Brown a few pieces at a time in butter in Dutch oven or 10″ heavy skillet. Remove from pan.

Blend flour with the pan drippings. Stir in chicken broth, instant minced onion, tarragon, white pepper and garlic powder; stir to blend. Add chicken; cover and simmer 25 minutes. Remove chicken to hot platter.

Add sour cream to pan and stir just until heated, do not boil. Check seasonings, adding more salt and white pepper, if necessary. Spoon some of the sauce over chicken. Pour remaining sauce into gravy boat or small bowl. Makes 4 servings. Double recipe for 8 servings.

CHICKEN PAPRIKA

Paprika and sour cream team for a delicious blending of flavors

2 (3 lb.) broiler-fryers	1 tblsp. instant minced onion
¾ c. flour	1 tblsp. paprika
2½ tsp. salt	⅛ tsp. garlic powder
4 tblsp. butter or regular margarine	$\frac{1}{16}$ tsp. ground red pepper
1½ c. diced fresh tomatoes	1 c. dairy sour cream
2 tblsp. sweet pepper flakes	1 egg yolk, beaten
½ c. water	Fresh minced parsley
	Hot, cooked noodles

Cut chickens into serving-size pieces and dust with flour mixed with salt. Melt butter in large saucepan. Add chicken and brown lightly on all sides.

Add tomatoes, pepper flakes, water, instant minced onion, paprika, garlic powder and red pepper. Bring to a boil, reduce heat. Cover and simmer until chicken is tender, about 30 to 40 minutes. Remove chicken to serving dish.

Mix sour cream with egg yolk and add to liquid left in saucepan. Heat but do not boil. Pour over chicken. Garnish with parsley. Serve with hot, cooked noodles. Makes 6 to 8 servings.

HERBED CHICKEN DELICIOUS

The chicken livers help to make this chicken dish unforgettable

2 tsp. salt
1 tsp. poultry seasoning
¼ tsp. pepper
⅛ tsp. garlic powder
1 (2½ lb.) broiler-fryer, cut up
3 tblsp. salad oil

½ lb. chicken livers, halved
1 (1 lb.) can tomatoes
½ c. water
3 tblsp. flour
¼ c. water

Combine salt, poultry seasoning, pepper and garlic powder; rub on all sides of chicken pieces.

Heat oil in large skillet. Add chicken, a few pieces at a time, and brown about 5 minutes on each side. Brown chicken livers; set aside.

Return chicken pieces to skillet. Add tomatoes and ½ c. water; bring to a boil. Reduce heat, cover and simmer 20 minutes. Add chicken livers and simmer 10 minutes longer, or until chicken is fork tender. Remove chicken to platter and keep warm.

Blend flour with ¼ c. water. Stir some of the hot liquid from skillet into flour mixture, then add to skillet. Cook and stir 1 minute, until thickened. Spoon over chicken. Makes 4 servings. Double recipe for 8 servings.

TARRAGON FRIED CHICKEN

Tarragon has long been a favorite herb with chicken

½ c. flour
1 tsp. salt
¼ tsp. pepper
1 tsp. dried tarragon leaves,
    crumbled

⅛ tsp. ground ginger
1 (2½ lb.) broiler-fryer,
    cut up
⅓ c. evaporated milk
½ c. shortening

Combine flour, salt, pepper, tarragon and ginger. Dip each chicken piece in evaporated milk, then coat with flour mixture.

Fry in hot shortening in large skillet, turning pieces frequently to brown on all sides.

Transfer chicken to shallow baking pan, and bake in hot oven (400°) 20 to 30 minutes, or until chicken is tender. Makes 4 servings. Double recipe for 8 servings.

CHICKEN MARENGO

This dish is also good reheated . . . just serve with hot rice

¼ c. flour

1 tsp. parsley flakes, finely crumbled

½ tsp. dried thyme leaves, finely crumbled

½ tsp. dried savory leaves, finely crumbled

1 tsp. salt

¼ tsp. pepper

1 (3 lb.) broiler-fryer, cut up

¼ c. salad oil

1 (13¾ oz.) can chicken broth

1 (6 oz.) can tomato paste

1 (8 oz.) can sliced mushrooms, drained

½ c. chopped onion

Place flour, parsley, thyme, savory, salt and pepper in plastic or paper bag.

Wash chicken, do not dry. Add to bag with seasonings, a few pieces at a time, and toss to coat all pieces well with flour mixture.

Heat oil in 10″ heavy skillet. Add chicken and fry until browned. Drain off excess fat.

Mix chicken broth with tomato paste; pour over chicken in skillet. Add mushrooms and onion. Cover and cook over medium-low heat about 30 to 45 minutes, or until chicken is very tender. Serve with sauce remaining in skillet. Makes 4 servings.

CHICKEN FRICASSEE WITH DUMPLINGS

Try these dumplings with other favorite chicken dishes too

¼ c. flour
1 tsp. salt
¼ tsp. pepper
6 chicken legs and thighs
2 tblsp. butter or regular
    margarine
3 c. water
1 carrot, finely shredded
1 tsp. salt
1 tblsp. instant minced onion
½ tsp. dried thyme leaves,
    crumbled

½ tsp. dried marjoram leaves,
    crumbled
½ tsp. dried rosemary leaves,
    crumbled
1 bay leaf
¼ lb. fresh mushrooms, sliced
2 c. all-purpose buttermilk
    biscuit mix
2 tblsp. Toasted Sesame Seeds
    (recipe follows)
2 eggs, well beaten
⅓ c. milk

Combine flour with 1 tsp. salt and pepper. Dredge chicken with seasoned flour. Melt butter in Dutch oven. Add chicken and sauté until golden.

Add water, carrot, 1 tsp. salt, instant minced onion, thyme, marjoram, rosemary and bay leaf. Bring to boiling point; reduce heat, cover and simmer 15 minutes.

Add mushrooms and cook 15 minutes longer.

Meanwhile, combine biscuit mix with Toasted Sesame Seeds, eggs and milk; stir well with fork. Drop by tablespoonfuls onto chicken. Cover and cook 12 minutes without lifting top from Dutch oven. Serve immediately. Makes 6 servings.

Toasted Sesame Seeds: Place sesame seeds in shallow pan. Bake in moderate oven (350°) about 20 minutes, or until seeds are a pale brown. (Do not overbrown.)

CHICKEN GENOESE-STYLE

Even ordinary chicken seems special prepared in this manner

2 tblsp. salad oil	1 tblsp. parsley flakes
6 chicken legs and thighs, disjointed	½ tsp. dried rosemary leaves, crumbled
¾ c. dry red wine	½ tsp. salt
1½ c. chicken broth	⅛ tsp. instant minced garlic
¼ c. tomato paste	1/16 tsp. pepper
¼ c. instant minced onion	1 medium tomato, diced

Heat oil in large skillet. Add chicken and sauté until golden, about 10 minutes. Drain excess fat from skillet.

Pour wine over chicken. Cook, uncovered, over low heat until wine has evaporated, about 15 minutes.

Add chicken broth, tomato paste, instant minced onion, parsley, rosemary, salt, instant minced garlic, pepper and tomato. Continue cooking, uncovered, over low heat 20 minutes or until chicken is tender. Add more water or broth if needed (sauce should be very thick). Makes 6 servings.

SOUTHERN FRIED CHICKEN

Serve chicken in individual baskets for a television dinner

¼ c. flour	1 tsp. salt
2 tblsp. cornmeal	½ tsp. pepper
2 tsp. onion powder	1 (3 lb.) broiler-fryer, cut up
2 tsp. Fines Herbes (see Index)	¼ c. salad oil

Place flour, cornmeal, onion powder, Fines Herbes, salt and pepper in plastic or paper bag.

Wash chicken, but do not dry. Add to bag with seasonings, a few pieces at a time, and toss to coat all pieces well with flour mixture.

Heat oil in a 10″ heavy skillet. Add chicken and brown on all sides. Place chicken in 11×7×1½″ baking pan.

Bake in moderate oven (350°) 30 to 45 minutes, or until tender and crisp. Makes 4 servings. Double recipe and bake in large shallow pan for 8 servings.

PERFECT PARTY POTLUCK

Tarragon leaves are accented in this extra-special chicken dish

1 (4 lb.) stewing chicken,
  cut up
Water
⅔ c. raw regular rice
2 tblsp. butter
1 c. coarsely chopped green
  pepper
1 c. finely chopped celery
1 (8½ oz.) can water chestnuts,
  drained and sliced
1 (4 oz.) can mushrooms,
  drained

1 (4 oz.) jar pimientos, drained
  and chopped
½ c. slivered almonds
1 tsp. salt
1 tsp. dried tarragon leaves,
  crumbled
½ tsp. pepper
2 (10½ oz.) cans condensed
  cream of chicken soup

Simmer chicken in water to cover until tender, about 2½ to 3 hours. Remove chicken, saving broth (you will need 1⅓ c.). Cool chicken; remove skin and bones and cut in bite-size pieces (you should have 3½ c.).

Combine chicken broth with rice in large saucepan. Bring to a boil; stir. Cover tightly; reduce heat and simmer 12 to 15 minutes, or until rice is tender and all liquid is absorbed.

Melt butter in large skillet; add green pepper, celery, water chestnuts, mushrooms, pimientos, nuts, salt, tarragon and pepper. Stir-fry until green pepper and celery are tender. Add chicken, rice and soup. Heat through. Makes 6 servings.

HERBED BRAISED CHICKEN

If you wish, thicken the cooking liquid for a flavorful gravy

½ c. flour	½ tsp. celery salt
1½ tsp. dried thyme leaves, crumbled	⅛ tsp. pepper
1 tsp. paprika	1 (3- to 4-lb.) broiler-fryer, cut up
1 tsp. salt	¼ c. shortening
½ tsp. onion salt	1 c. water

Place flour, thyme, paprika, salt, onion salt, celery salt and pepper in plastic or paper bag. Add chicken pieces, a few at a time, and toss to coat well with flour mixture.

Heat shortening in skillet; add chicken and fry 20 to 25 minutes, turning to brown on all sides. Add water; cover and simmer 25 to 30 minutes. Makes 4 servings. Double recipe for 8 servings.

GULF COAST CHICKEN

You'll like this interesting combination—shrimp and chicken

2 c. dairy sour cream	4 large chicken breasts, cut in lengthwise halves
2 tblsp. milk	1 c. corn flake crumbs
¼ tsp. dried tarragon leaves, crumbled	1 c. cooked cleaned shrimp, split in lengthwise halves
½ tsp. dried rosemary leaves, crumbled	¼ c. sliced ripe olives
1 tsp. salt	1 tsp. paprika
¼ tsp. pepper	

Combine sour cream and milk; stir to blend. Add tarragon, rosemary, salt and pepper, and mix.

Dip chicken in sour cream mixture, then roll in corn flake crumbs. Place in large shallow baking pan. Bake in moderate oven (350°) 40 minutes; turn and bake 15 minutes longer.

Add shrimp and olives to remaining sour cream mixture and

spoon over chicken. Sprinkle with paprika, and bake 10 to 15 minutes more. Makes 8 servings.

SCALLOPED CHICKEN

A colorful main dish you'll want to serve often. Cream sauce seasoned with tarragon and rosemary adds character

2 c. chopped cooked chicken
1 (4 oz.) can sliced mushrooms, drained
1 (4 oz.) jar pimientos, drained and chopped
1 c. cooked spaghetti
1 (10½ oz.) can condensed cream of celery soup
½ c. light cream

½ tsp. salt
⅛ tsp. pepper
¼ tsp. dried tarragon leaves, finely crumbled
¼ tsp. dried rosemary leaves, finely crumbled
2 tblsp. butter
½ c. grated Parmesan cheese

Combine chicken, mushrooms, pimientos and spaghetti.

Mix together soup, light cream, salt, pepper, tarragon and rosemary; add to chicken mixture, blending well. Spoon into 2-qt. casserole. Dot with butter and sprinkle with cheese.

Bake in moderate oven (350°) 20 to 30 minutes, or until brown and bubbling. Makes 4 servings. Double recipe and bake in 4-qt. casserole for 8 servings.

ISLAND BROILED CHICKEN

Corn on the cob and sliced tomatoes are good accompaniments

2 (3 lb.) broiler-fryers, quartered
½ c. soy sauce
¼ c. water
⅓ c. salad oil
2 tblsp. instant minced onion

2 tblsp. sesame seeds
1 tblsp. sugar
1 tsp. ground ginger
¾ tsp. salt
½ tsp. instant minced garlic
⅛ tsp. ground red pepper

Place chicken in a tight-fitting bowl or double-lined plastic bag; combine soy sauce, water, oil, instant minced onion, sesame seeds, sugar, ginger, salt, instant minced garlic and red pepper; mix well. Pour over chicken, cover and marinate in refrigerator 12 hours or longer, turning occasionally.

Remove chicken from marinade. Arrange chicken on rack in pan under preheated broiler. Broil, turning and basting frequently with marinade until chicken is done, about 45 minutes. Or broil on rack over hot charcoal, turning and basting frequently with marinade, 45 minutes, or until done. Makes 8 servings.

OVEN-BARBECUED CHICKEN

This chicken is also delicious cooked outdoors on the grill

2 (2 lb.) broiler-fryers, cut in halves
1 c. tomato juice
1 c. chili sauce
2 tsp. Worcestershire sauce

2 tblsp. Tarragon Wine Vinegar or red wine vinegar
1 tsp. chili powder
½ tsp. garlic salt

Lay chicken halves skin side up in broiler pan. Bake in hot oven (400°) 30 minutes.

Combine tomato juice, chili sauce, Worcestershire sauce, vinegar, chili powder and garlic salt. Pour over chicken; bake 30 minutes longer, or until chicken is tender, basting frequently with sauce. Makes 4 servings. Double recipe for 8 servings.

OVEN-FRIED CHICKEN

A carefree way to cook chicken. Perfect with baked potatoes

¾ c. flour
1 tsp. poultry seasoning
1 tsp. salt
¼ tsp. pepper

1 (2½ lb.) broiler-fryer, cut up
3 tblsp. butter

Place flour, poultry seasoning, salt and pepper in plastic or paper bag. Add chicken, a few pieces at a time, and toss to coat pieces well with flour mixture.

Place chicken in greased shallow baking pan; dot with butter. Bake in moderate oven (375°) 50 to 60 minutes, or until chicken is brown and tender. Makes 4 servings. Double recipe for 8 servings.

QUICK CHICKEN CROQUETTES

These are also tasty prepared with leftover cooked turkey

4 c. finely chopped cooked chicken
1 c. soft bread crumbs
1 c. cooked rice
1 c. mayonnaise
1 tsp. salt
¼ tsp. pepper
½ tsp. Savory Meat Blend (see Index)
1 tsp. parsley flakes, finely crumbled
1 c. cornmeal
Parsley Sauce (see Index)

Mix chicken with bread crumbs, rice, mayonnaise, salt, pepper, Savory Meat Blend and parsley. Form into cone-shaped croquettes, using about ½ c. mixture for each. Roll croquettes in cornmeal to coat well.

Place on greased baking sheet and bake in hot oven (400°) 20 minutes. Serve with Parsley Sauce. Makes 8 servings.

CHICKEN MUSHROOM NEWBURG

For a special luncheon dish, spoon over toasted English muffins

3 egg yolks, slightly beaten
1 c. light cream
½ tsp. salt
½ tsp. poultry seasoning
¹⁄₁₆ tsp. pepper
½ c. sliced fresh mushrooms
2 tblsp. butter
2 c. cubed cooked chicken
¼ c. chicken stock or dry sherry
Toast or patty shells
Paprika

Combine egg yolks and light cream in top of double boiler. Add salt, poultry seasoning and pepper. Cook over hot water (not boiling), stirring constantly, until mixture is consistency of custard.

Sauté mushrooms in melted butter in skillet.

Add chicken, stock and sautéed mushrooms to sauce; blend well and cook about 3 minutes longer. Serve immediately on toast. Garnish with paprika. Makes 6 servings.

SAGE CHICKEN LIVERS

Why not serve this as the main entree for a holiday brunch

¼ c. butter or regular margarine
2 lbs. chicken livers, halved
¾ tsp. dried sage leaves, crumbled
¼ tsp. salt
⅛ tsp. pepper
2 tblsp. dry marsala or sherry
Toast points (optional)

Melt butter in medium skillet. Add chicken livers, sage, salt and pepper. Cook, stirring constantly, 5 minutes. Remove chicken livers from pan; set aside and keep warm.

Add wine to liquid in pan. Cook, stirring constantly, 3 minutes. Pour over chicken livers. Serve on toast points, if desired. Makes 4 to 6 servings.

RAISIN AND NUT STUFFING

Good with roast chicken . . . just bake in a 3-quart casserole

3 qts. toasted bread cubes
¾ c. onion flakes
¼ c. parsley flakes
1 tsp. poultry seasoning
1 tblsp. celery seeds
1 tblsp. salt
¼ tsp. pepper
1½ c. seedless raisins
½ c. chopped walnuts
½ c. melted butter or regular margarine
1 c. apple cider

Combine bread cubes, onion flakes, parsley flakes, poultry seasoning, celery seeds, salt, pepper, raisins and walnuts; mix together well. Stir in melted butter and cider. Makes enough stuffing for neck region and body cavity of a 10- to 12-lb. turkey.

QUICK HERBED TURKEY STUFFING

Serve stuffing in a large bowl with gravy spooned over it

2 c. chicken stock
1 c. butter or regular
  margarine
2 tblsp. instant minced onion

1 tsp. poultry seasoning
½ tsp. instant minced garlic
2 (8 oz.) pkgs. herb-seasoned
  stuffing

Combine chicken stock and butter in large saucepan. Heat until butter is melted. Stir in instant minced onion, poultry seasoning and instant minced garlic, then add stuffing. Mix lightly. Makes enough stuffing for neck region and body cavity of a 10- to 12-lb. turkey.

HERBED SESAME SEED STUFFING

When serving stuffing, garnish with cherry tomatoes and parsley

3 qts. toasted bread cubes
1 c. Toasted Sesame Seeds (see
  Index)
⅓ c. parsley flakes
¼ c. instant minced onion
1 tsp. salt

2 tsp. poultry seasoning
¼ tsp. pepper
1 c. butter or regular
  margarine
1 c. turkey stock or water

Combine bread cubes, sesame seeds, parsley, instant minced onion, salt, poultry seasoning, pepper and butter in large mixing bowl. Mix well. Add turkey stock; mix lightly, but thoroughly. Makes enough stuffing for neck region and body cavity of a 15-lb. turkey.

HERBED CORN BREAD STUFFING

This dressing is also a good accompaniment to roast pork loin

7 c. toasted white bread cubes
4 c. toasted corn bread crumbs
¾ c. onion flakes
2 tblsp. parsley flakes
2 tsp. poultry seasoning
2 tsp. salt
½ tsp. pepper
1 c. melted butter or regular margarine
¾ c. turkey stock or water
3 eggs, beaten

Combine bread cubes, corn bread crumbs, onion flakes, parsley, poultry seasoning, salt, pepper and butter in large mixing bowl. Mix lightly, but well. Add turkey stock and eggs. Mix lightly, but thoroughly. Makes enough stuffing for neck region and body cavity of a 15-lb. turkey.

HOLIDAY SPECIAL STUFFING

This expertly seasoned stuffing will be the center of attention at your very special holiday dinner

4 c. cooked rice
4 c. toasted bread cubes
4 eggs, slightly beaten
1 c. diced cooked ham
⅔ c. chopped pimiento-stuffed olives
½ tsp. salt
1 tsp. ground sage
1 tsp. ground marjoram
½ tsp. pepper
½ tsp. celery salt
¼ tsp. instant minced garlic
¼ c. parsley flakes
⅓ c. onion flakes
½ c. celery flakes

Combine all ingredients, and mix together lightly. Makes enough stuffing for neck region and body cavity of a 12- to 15-lb. turkey.

HERBED LIVERWURST STUFFING

Quite an unusual flavor combination . . . a real crowd-pleaser

½ lb. liverwurst
2 qts. toasted bread cubes
⅓ c. instant minced onion
¼ c. celery flakes
3 tblsp. parsley flakes
1 tsp. salt

1 tsp. poultry seasoning
⅛ tsp. pepper
⅔ c. melted butter or regular
    margarine
½ c. turkey stock

Put liverwurst through food chopper, using coarse blade. Mix with bread cubes, instant minced onion, celery flakes, parsley flakes, salt, poultry seasoning, pepper, butter and turkey stock. Makes enough stuffing for neck region and body cavity of a 10- to 12-lb. turkey.

APPLE BREAD STUFFING IN CASSEROLE

Delicious with roast duckling, chicken, turkey or pork loin

6 c. toasted bread cubes
2 c. sliced apples
½ c. onion flakes
¼ c. celery flakes
¾ c. water
¼ c. melted butter or regular
    margarine

1½ tsp. poultry seasoning
1 tsp. salt
1 tsp. parsley flakes
¾ to 1 c. chicken stock or water
1 tblsp. butter or regular
    margarine

Combine bread cubes and apples in large mixing bowl.

Mix onion and celery flakes with water; let stand 5 minutes, then sauté in ¼ c. melted butter about 5 minutes. Add to bread-apple mixture along with poultry seasoning, salt, parsley and chicken stock. Mix well. Place in buttered 2-qt. casserole. Dot with 1 tblsp. butter.

Cover and bake in moderate oven (375°) 30 minutes. Makes 8 servings.

Colorful Vegetables with a Difference

In our zealous pursuit of vitamins and minerals, we sometimes forget that vegetables don't *have* to be just cooked quickly in a little water and served plain. You can serve vegetables in an infinite variety of dressed-up ways and also preserve vitamins and minerals. Have you neglected cream sauces, garnishes, au gratin combinations, scalloped vegetable dishes, or the combining of complementary vegetables?

Even canned vegetables gain status when you add a pinch of marjoram, basil, parsley or savory to the liquid when you heat them.

And here comes Herb Butter (see Index) to the rescue— really, it is such a help. If you're in the habit of adding a pat of butter to your vegetables, try Herb Butter instead of plain—it's the quick and easy way to get the herb flavor without worrying about adding too little or too much seasoning.

You can improve any kind of potatoes (except French fries) by adding an herb—parsley, sage, thyme, rosemary or marjoram.

If your family doesn't go for the "smelly vegetables" (cabbage, cauliflower, broccoli and Brussels sprouts), try adding 2 tablespoons of herb wine vinegar to the water in which they're cooked, then serve a cruet of the same vinegar to sprinkle over the vegetable at the table. It may even convert the children to these healthful vegetables. Dill Wine Vinegar is great with cauliflower, Basil Wine Vinegar with cabbage, Burnet or Garlic Wine Vinegar with broccoli, and Chive Wine Vinegar with Brussels sprouts. (See Index for the above herb wine vinegars.)

Pickled beets are out of this world when you make them with Mint Wine Vinegar—½ cup for 4 servings. And even if you have a favorite recipe for baked beans, try making them with 2 tablespoons of Basil Wine Vinegar and ¼ cup of Herb

Mustard to 1 pound (2 cups) of dried beans (see Index for recipes).

Basil, dill, fennel, marjoram, orégano, parsley, rosemary, savory, tarragon and thyme all blend well with vegetables. Don't forget Herb Salt, Salad Herbs and Fines Herbes, either. For any onion dish, orégano is the better half of seasoning.

BASIL BUTTERED ASPARAGUS

Also a delicious way to serve fresh asparagus in season

2 tblsp. butter or regular margarine	Salt to taste
	Pepper to taste
¼ tsp. dried basil leaves, crushed	2 (10 oz.) pkgs. frozen asparagus, cooked

Melt butter in small saucepan. Add basil, salt and pepper, and stir to mix. Pour over cooked asparagus. Serve hot. Makes 6 servings.

SNAPPY GREEN BEANS

Herb Mustard adds just the right tang to these green beans

1 (10 oz.) pkg. frozen green beans	1¼ c. light cream
	½ tsp. salt
3 slices bacon	2 tsp. Herb Mustard (see Index)
2 tblsp. cornstarch	

Cook green beans according to package directions, but omitting salt.

Dice bacon. Cook in 1-qt. saucepan over low heat until crisp and brown. Remove from pan; drain, reserving fat. Crumble bacon. Return 2 tblsp. fat to saucepan.

Mix cornstarch with cream, salt and Herb Mustard; blend into fat in saucepan. Cook over medium heat, stirring constantly, until smooth. Add bacon and beans; heat through. Makes 4 servings. Double recipe for 8 servings.

ITALIAN GREEN BEANS WITH NOODLES

Basil and orégano give this dish a unique flavor

2 c. uncooked fine noodles	1 tsp. salt
1 c. finely chopped onion	½ tsp. celery salt
¼ c. butter or regular margarine	½ tsp. dried basil leaves, crumbled
2 (9 oz.) pkgs. frozen Italian green beans	½ tsp. dried orégano leaves, crumbled
1 (8 oz.) can sliced mushrooms, drained	

Cook noodles according to package directions; drain.

Sauté onion in melted butter in large skillet until tender (do not brown). Add cooked noodles, frozen beans, mushrooms, salt, celery salt, basil and orégano. Cover and simmer 10 to 15 minutes or until beans are tender, stirring occasionally. Makes 6 to 8 servings.

LIMAS WITH ZIPPY SAUCE

Even people who dislike limas will find this hard to resist

1 (10 oz.) pkg. frozen lima beans	⅛ tsp. ground marjoram
1 tblsp. cornstarch	2 tblsp. butter or regular margarine
¾ c. light cream	½ c. shredded sharp process cheese
¼ tsp. dried thyme leaves, finely crumbled	

Cook beans as directed on package; drain.

While beans are cooking, prepare sauce. Place cornstarch in saucepan; gradually blend in cream to make a smooth paste. Add thyme and marjoram and cook, stirring constantly, until thickened. Add butter and cheese, stirring to blend. Add cooked beans and heat through. Makes 4 servings. Double recipe for 8 servings.

GLAZED CARROTS

Prepare a colorful vegetable plate by combining with fresh peas

6 to 8 tender young carrots	¼ c. honey
1 tblsp. butter	½ tsp. mint flakes, crushed

Peel carrots and cut in pieces 2″ long. Cook rapidly in a little boiling salted water until tender; drain.

Meanwhile, melt butter in saucepan; add honey and mint and heat. Add carrots; toss to glaze and heat through. Makes 4 servings. Double recipe for 8 servings.

BEST YET BAKED BEANS

A quick luncheon dish to serve your children during the winter

1 c. diced celery	2 (1 lb.) cans pork and beans
½ c. chopped green pepper	with tomato sauce
½ c. chopped chives	⅓ c. molasses
2 tblsp. salad oil	6 slices bacon (optional)
½ c. ketchup	

Sauté celery, green pepper and chives in hot oil in skillet. Combine with ketchup, beans and molasses. Turn into 2-qt. casserole. Top with bacon slices, if you wish.

Bake in moderate oven (350°) 1 hour and 15 minutes. Makes 6 servings.

HONOLULU BAKED BEANS

Leftover baked ham helps to make this casserole special

2 (1 lb.) cans pork and beans	1 c. drained pineapple chunks
with tomato sauce	¼ tsp. aniseeds
2 c. cubed cooked ham	

Combine beans with ham, pineapple and aniseeds in 2-qt. casserole.

Bake in moderate oven (350°) 1 hour, until hot and bubbly. Makes 6 servings.

SPICED BEETS

Choose this spicy vegetable to accompany any meat or fish

1 (1 lb.) can sliced or diced beets	½ tsp. onion salt
	¼ tsp. ground ginger
1½ tblsp. cider vinegar	⅛ tsp. dried rosemary leaves
1 tsp. sugar	⅛ tsp. ground cloves

Place beets with their liquid in saucepan. Add vinegar, sugar, onion salt, ginger, rosemary and cloves. Heat 3 to 5 minutes. Serve hot. Makes 4 servings. Double recipe for 8 servings.

MINTED BEETS

The perfect choice to serve with roast pork and cabbage

1 (1 lb.) jar pickled sliced beets	1 tsp. mint flakes, crumbled
	½ tsp. sugar

Drain liquid from beets into small saucepan. Add mint and sugar; bring to a boil. Reduce heat and simmer 5 minutes. Add beets and simmer until heated. Makes 4 servings. Double recipe for 8 servings.

CABBAGE AUSTRALIA

This tangy dish is good with either corned beef or ham

1 medium firm head cabbage	½ c. Chive or Dill Wine
2 c. water	Vinegar (see Index) or white
1 tsp. salt	wine vinegar
1 tsp. sugar	4 tblsp. butter

Wash cabbage and discard any wilted leaves. Cut in four wedges; remove core.

Pour water in 2-qt. saucepan. Add salt, sugar and vinegar.

Bring to a boil, gently drop in cabbage wedges. Cook just until cabbage is tender, 10 to 15 minutes. Drain and serve, topping each wedge with 1 tblsp. butter. Makes 4 servings. Double recipe for 8 servings.

HERBED CREOLE CABBAGE

Orégano adds spark to this unusual vegetable combination

9 c. shredded cabbage	1½ tsp. sugar
1 (1 lb.) can tomatoes	¾ tsp. dried orégano leaves,
¼ c. sweet pepper flakes	crumbled
2 tblsp. instant minced onion	2 tsp. lemon juice
2½ tsp. salt	

Add cabbage to medium saucepan containing ½" boiling water; cover and cook 10 minutes. Drain.

Combine tomatoes, sweet pepper flakes, instant minced onion, salt, sugar and orégano in medium saucepan. Simmer, uncovered, 15 minutes.

Add cabbage and lemon juice to tomato mixture; heat well. Makes 8 servings.

BRAISED CELERY

If you've never served celery as a hot vegetable, try this

2 bunches celery	¼ tsp. dried basil leaves, finely
2 tblsp. butter	crumbled
1 (10½ oz.) can condensed	Fresh parsley
beef consommé	

Separate celery into branches; clean and cut each branch in 2" pieces.

Melt butter in large skillet; add celery. Add consommé and basil; cover and simmer over low heat 25 minutes, until celery is tender but firm. Sprinkle with minced fresh parsley. Makes 4 servings. Double recipe for 8 servings.

MEXICAN CORN PUDDING

This hot vegetable will appeal to the youngsters in your family

1 (16 or 17 oz.) can cream-
    style corn
2 eggs, well beaten
4 pimientos, finely chopped
⅓ c. finely chopped green
    pepper

½ tsp. salt
⅛ tsp. pepper
¼ tsp. dried orégano leaves,
    finely crumbled
2 or 3 drops Tabasco sauce

Combine corn, eggs, pimientos, green pepper, salt, pepper, orégano and Tabasco; mix well. Pour into buttered 1-qt. shallow casserole.

Bake in moderate oven (350°) 30 to 40 minutes, or until knife inserted halfway between center and edge comes out clean. Makes 4 servings. Make 2 casseroles for 8 servings.

FRENCH PEAS

This delicious combination is elegant enough for company

2 c. shelled fresh peas (about 3
    lbs.)
¼ tsp. mint flakes, finely
    crumbled

1 tsp. salt
1 tblsp. Herb Butter (see Index)

Cook fresh peas with mint and salt in 1" boiling water until tender, 8 to 10 minutes. Drain. Add Herb Butter and toss gently. Serve immediately. Makes 4 servings. Double recipe for 8 servings.

NOTE: Canned peas can be substituted for fresh ones. Use 1 (1 lb.) can and cook long enough to just heat through.

SAVORY MASHED POTATOES

These mashed potatoes will soon become a favorite family recipe

¼ tsp. dried thyme leaves,
   finely crumbled
2 tblsp. chopped fresh chives
½ tsp. salt

3 tblsp. butter
3 c. hot mashed potatoes
1 tblsp. Herb Butter (see
   Index)

Whip thyme, chives, salt and butter into mashed potatoes. Pile into serving dish; make a small hollow in center and fill with the Herb Butter. Serve immediately. Makes 4 servings. Double recipe for 8 servings.

SOUTHERN FRIED POTATOES AND ONIONS

So good with a cheese omelet and buttered English muffins

¼ c. butter
4 medium potatoes, pared and
   sliced
2 crisp-cooked slices bacon,
   crumbled

4 medium onions, sliced
1 tsp. salt
⅛ tsp. pepper
2 tblsp. minced fresh parsley

Melt butter in 10″ heavy skillet. Add potatoes, bacon, onions, salt, pepper and parsley. Fry until potatoes and onions are tender, crisp and brown. Makes 4 to 6 servings.

BAKED STUFFED POTATOES

Plain baked potatoes will seem ordinary after you've tried these

4 large baking potatoes
¼ c. light cream
1 egg, well beaten
1 c. grated sharp process cheese
1 tsp. salt

2 tblsp. butter
1 tsp. Fines Herbes (see Index)
2 tblsp. melted butter
Paprika

Scrub, then bake potatoes in hot oven (400°) 45 to 50 minutes, until almost done but still firm.

Cut each potato in half lengthwise. With a teaspoon, carefully scoop out insides, leaving enough potato in the shells to hold their shape. Mash potatoes well, blending in light cream, egg, cheese, salt, 2 tblsp. butter and Fines Herbes. Pile mixture lightly into shells. Drizzle melted butter over top, then sprinkle with paprika.

Place potatoes under broiler for a few minutes to brown and heat through. Makes 8 servings.

PARSLIED POTATOES

Take your choice of herbs—parsley or tarragon—both are good

20 small new potatoes   ½ tsp. salt
  (about 1½" in diameter)   1 tblsp. parsley flakes, finely
¼ c. butter or regular margarine   crumbled

Boil potatoes in water to cover until tender. Carefully remove skins.

Meanwhile, melt butter in small saucepan and add salt and parsley. Let stand so parsley can soften and soak up butter.

Roll potatoes in butter mixture and serve. Makes about 4 to 5 servings.

HERB POTATO CAKES

A supper dish that is tasty and uses those leftover potatoes

2 c. salad oil   1 tsp. salt
2 c. cold mashed potatoes   1 tblsp. chopped fresh chives
2 eggs, slightly beaten   1 tblsp. chopped fresh parsley

Heat oil in deep saucepan or deep fat fryer.

Combine potatoes, eggs, salt, chives and parsley; mix well. Drop by spoonfuls into hot oil and fry to a golden brown, about 5 minutes. Drain on paper towels. Keep warm in very slow oven (200°) while you fry remaining cakes. Makes about 2 dozen small cakes.

SCALLOPED SPINACH WITH MARJORAM

It's the herb sauce that gives spinach its peppery taste—good

1 lb. fresh young spinach leaves
2 tsp. cornstarch
½ c. light cream
½ tsp. sugar
½ tsp. salt

¼ tsp. pepper
¼ tsp. dried marjoram leaves,
   crumbled
1 tblsp. butter or regular
   margarine

Wash spinach thoroughly in running cold water; drain and tear in small pieces.

Mix cornstarch with cream, sugar, salt, pepper and marjoram; stir until smooth. Add spinach and mix well. Place in 3-qt. casserole; dot with butter.

Bake in moderate oven (350°) about 30 minutes. Makes 4 servings.

ZUCCHINI ITALIENNE

The seasonings—salt, basil and garlic salt—make the difference

2 large zucchini (about 1 lb.)
1 medium onion, coarsely
   chopped
1 (1 lb.) can tomato wedges
¼ tsp. dried basil leaves, finely
   crumbled

1 tsp. salt
¼ tsp. garlic salt
½ c. fresh bread crumbs
2 tblsp. melted butter
2 tblsp. grated Parmesan cheese

Cut ends from unpeeled zucchini; cut in cubes (you should have about 4 c.). Mix with onion, tomatoes, basil, salt and garlic salt. Spoon into 2-qt. casserole.

Toss bread crumbs with melted butter. Sprinkle over mixture in casserole. Top with Parmesan cheese.

Bake in moderate oven (350°) 45 minutes, or until zucchini is tender. Makes 4 to 6 servings.

WALNUT-STUFFED SQUASH

A combination of sage and thyme makes this dish different

3 large acorn squash	2 c. unseasoned croutons
¼ c. melted butter or regular margarine	1 c. coarsely chopped toasted walnuts
½ tsp. ground sage	1 (6 oz.) can chopped
⅛ tsp. ground thyme	mushrooms, drained
⅛ tsp. pepper	1 tblsp. melted butter or
¼ tsp. salt	regular margarine

Wash squash and cut in lengthwise halves. With a spoon scrape out seeds and stringy portion. Place cut side down in shallow baking pan. Pour in boiling water to a depth of ¼". Bake in hot oven (400°) 30 minutes.

In the meantime, blend together ¼ c. melted butter, sage, thyme, pepper and salt.

In large bowl combine croutons and walnuts. Add mushrooms and seasoned butter; toss lightly to blend.

Remove cooked squash from pan and turn cut side up; fill with stuffing. Brush cut surface with 1 tblsp. melted butter.

Place in baking pan and bake in moderate oven (375°) 40 minutes, or until squash is tender. Makes 6 servings.

BAKED TOMATO SURPRISE

These will make a hit whether it's brunch or supper

6 large firm, ripe tomatoes	2 tblsp. cooking oil
8 eggs	1 c. shredded Cheddar
½ tsp. salt	cheese
¼ tsp. dried basil leaves, crumbled	1 c. bread cubes (½")
	Chopped fresh parsley

Cut tops off tomatoes. Remove centers with a spoon and reserve. Chop enough tomato flesh to make 1 c. Turn tomato shells upside down on a paper towel to drain.

Beat eggs slightly with salt and basil. Pour egg mixture into hot oil in large skillet over medium heat. Reduce heat to low. When eggs begin to set at bottom and sides, push them back with pancake turner to allow uncooked eggs to flow to bottom of pan. Cook until eggs are still slightly moist. Break eggs up into small pieces. Combine eggs, cheese, bread cubes and reserved tomato. Spoon mixture into tomato shells. Place tomatoes in 11×7×1½" baking dish.

Bake in moderate oven (375°) 15 minutes. Sprinkle with fresh parsley. Makes 6 servings.

SCALLOPED TOMATO CASSEROLE

A good accompaniment for fried or broiled fish fillets

1 tblsp. instant minced onion	6 large tomatoes, cut in 1"
1 tblsp. water	slices
½ c. fine cracker crumbs	1 tblsp. butter or regular
1 tsp. salt	margarine
½ tsp. ground thyme	½ c. shredded American cheese
¼ tsp. pepper	

Combine instant minced onion with water; let stand 5 minutes to soften. Combine onion, cracker crumbs, salt, thyme and pepper.

Place a layer of tomato slices in buttered 1½-qt. casserole; sprinkle with part of crumb mixture. Dot with butter. Repeat layers of tomatoes, crumbs and butter until all are used. Sprinkle top with cheese.

Bake in moderate oven (350°) 45 minutes. Makes 6 servings.

FRENCH FRIED VEGETABLES

So unusual, these vegetables will appeal to the whole family

2 peeled carrots, cut in ½"
    slices
2 or 3 branches celery, cut in
    1½" pieces
1 small head cauliflower,
    separated into flowerets
6 small onions, peeled

1 (8½ oz.) can water chestnuts,
    drained
1 egg, well beaten
½ c. cornmeal
Salad oil for deep-fat frying
½ tsp. Herb Salt (see Index)

Dip each vegetable in egg, then in cornmeal. Fry in deep hot oil (375°) about 8 minutes, or until vegetables are golden brown. Remove with tongs and drain on paper toweling. Serve hot, sprinkled with Herb Salt. Makes 6 servings.

NOTE: If you have a wire basket, use it for frying these vegetables; your work will be easier and the pieces will brown more evenly.

Fruit and Vegetable Salads

What better opportunity does a cook have to demonstrate her imagination and sense of variety than in the salad course? There are hot and cold salads, sweet and sour salads, tossed and molded salads, meat, vegetable and fruit salads—and herbs can add much to any of these.

Many fresh green herbs improve salads immeasurably when they are cut fine with shears or minced and tossed with the greens. Burnet, for example, with its fresh cucumber taste, makes a conversation piece of any salad in which it is used. Lovage is similar in taste to celery. Chives are like delicate, mild onions and so versatile. Thyme has a real herby taste; marjoram is pungent. Rosemary is rather pine-like in taste when used fresh, while tarragon has its own delightful personality. Fresh dill chopped and used in salads never fails to bring praise. Basil chopped fine and used sparingly is marvelous in any salad containing tomatoes. Mints are naturals for all fruit salads.

If you must substitute dried herbs, they should be steeped, or allowed to stand for an hour in vinegar or fresh lemon juice, to release their aromatic oils and to soften them. You can add herb flavors to salads also by using the herb wine vinegars, Herb French Dressing or the dried blends (see Index). If you're serving a dressing containing herbs with your salad, try not to use too many herbs in your other courses.

There are certain trios of herbs that go well together in all salads: burnet, chives and parsley; or chives, dill and basil; or tarragon, basil and orégano.

When you're serving any sweet salad, try rubbing the salad dish with fresh mint before placing the salad in the bowl. Sprigs of fresh green herbs make grand garnishes for salads too.

CUCUMBER MOUSSE

This pale green ring mold will add color to your buffet table

2 (3 oz.) pkgs. lime flavor
  gelatin
1 c. boiling water
1 c. cold water
2 unpeeled cucumbers, chopped
½ c. lemon juice
¼ c. Roquefort or blue cheese

1 c. heavy cream, whipped
1 c. dairy sour cream
½ tsp. salt
⅛ tsp. white pepper
2 tblsp. finely chopped fresh
  parsley

Dissolve gelatin in boiling water in large bowl.

Combine cold water, cucumbers, lemon juice and Roquefort cheese in blender. Blend 1 minute at high speed, or until cucumber is puréed. Add to gelatin in bowl. Blend in whipped cream, sour cream, salt, pepper and parsley.

Pour into lightly oiled 1½-qt. ring mold and chill until firm. Makes 8 servings.

HERBED TOMATO ASPIC

Favorite flavors—tomato juice, basil and chives—combine in this peppery salad. Good in summer with cold cuts and fruit

1 (24 oz.) can tomato juice
2 tblsp. lemon juice
2 tblsp. cider vinegar
½ tsp. salt
¼ tsp. dried basil leaves, finely
  crumbled

1 (3 oz.) pkg. lemon flavor
  gelatin
1 tblsp. finely chopped fresh
  chives
Special Aspic Dressing (see
  Index)

Heat tomato juice with lemon juice, vinegar, salt and basil. Remove from heat. Add lemon gelatin to hot juice; stir to dissolve. Add chives. Pour into 8″ square shallow pan and chill until firm.

Cut in 4″ squares and serve with Special Aspic Dressing. Makes 4 servings.

BASIL TOMATO ASPIC

Herbs in vinegar and salt give this salad plenty of zest

2 c. tomato juice

1 (3 oz.) pkg. lemon flavor
  gelatin

2 hard-cooked eggs, finely
  chopped

2 tblsp. finely chopped onion

½ c. finely chopped celery

½ green pepper, finely chopped

2 tblsp. Basil Wine Vinegar (see
  Index) or white wine vinegar

1 tsp. Herb Salt (see Index)

Heat tomato juice to boiling. Add lemon gelatin and stir to dissolve. Chill until partially set (consistency of unbeaten egg whites).

Add remaining ingredients; pour into 8″ square pan. Chill until firm. Makes 4 servings.

NOTE: Instead of an 8″ square pan, pour mixture into a 1-qt. ring mold and chill until set. Serve with seafood.

SHRIMP ASPIC

An excellent choice for a main dish on a hot summer day

2 c. water

½ tsp. dried orégano leaves,
  crumbled

½ tsp. salt

¼ c. sweet pepper flakes

1 lb. fresh shrimp (unshelled)

2 envelopes unflavored gelatin

1 c. tomato juice

2 tsp. instant minced onion

1 tblsp. lemon juice

½ tsp. salt

½ tsp. dried orégano leaves,
  crumbled

$\frac{1}{16}$ tsp. garlic powder

¼ tsp. pepper

1 c. dairy sour cream

1 c. diced celery

Salad greens (optional)

Sliced pimiento-stuffed olives
  (optional)

Place water in 2-qt. saucepan; add ½ tsp. orégano, ½ tsp. salt and sweet pepper flakes. Bring to a boil; reduce heat and simmer 5 minutes.

Wash shrimp but do not remove shells. Add to hot water

and simmer (do not boil) 6 to 8 minutes, only until shrimp turn pink. Remove from heat and drain, reserving liquid (you will need 1 c.). Peel, de-vein and coarsely chop shrimp; set aside.

Sprinkle gelatin over tomato juice; stir to dissolve. Heat shrimp water and add to softened gelatin. Stir in instant minced onion and let cool until mixture is the consistency of unbeaten egg whites. (To speed cooling, place bowl in a pan filled with ice cubes. Stir frequently.)

Blend together lemon juice, ½ tsp. salt, ½ tsp. orégano, garlic powder, pepper and sour cream; stir into gelatin along with the chopped shrimp and celery. Turn into oiled 5-c. mold. Refrigerate until firm. At serving time, unmold aspic onto serving plate; garnish with salad greens and olives, if desired. Makes 8 to 10 servings.

FROZEN FRUIT SALAD

Remove this salad from freezer 10 minutes before serving

1 (1 lb.) can pitted light sweet cherries, drained
1 (13½ oz.) can pineapple chunks, drained
1 c. canned seedless white grapes, drained
1 c. pecan halves

1 c. heavy cream, whipped
¼ c. mayonnaise
¼ c. Herb French Dressing (see Index)
¼ c. sugar
Lettuce

Combine cherries, pineapple chunks and grapes. Add pecans. Fold in whipped cream, mayonnaise, Herb French Dressing and sugar.

Pour into refrigerator tray; place in freezer and freeze until firm. Serve on lettuce. Makes 6 to 8 servings.

MINTED PEAR SALAD

Children will like this salad. Try also with peach halves

1 (1 lb.) can pear halves (6)	1 (3 oz.) pkg. cream cheese
2 tblsp. white vinegar	2 tblsp. heavy cream
⅛ tsp. peppermint extract	Lettuce
2 or 3 drops green food color	6 walnut halves

Drain pears, reserving liquid.

Combine pear liquid with vinegar, peppermint extract and food color. Add pears, and let stand in refrigerator until pears are tinted a pale green.

Soften cream cheese at room temperature, then blend with cream.

At serving time, drain pears and arrange cut side up on lettuce. Place a spoonful of cheese mixture in each pear half; top with a walnut half. Makes 6 servings.

ASPARAGUS SALAD

Herbs blend together to give asparagus special appeal

24 stalks asparagus	½ c. Herb French Dressing
1 hard-cooked egg, finely	(see Index)
chopped	Lettuce or spinach leaves
½ tsp. Salad Herbs (see Index)	

Cook asparagus in boiling water just until tender-crisp; drain.

Combine egg, Salad Herbs and Herb French Dressing; mix well. Pour over asparagus. Chill several hours to blend flavors.

To serve, arrange 6 stalks asparagus on lettuce or spinach leaves on each salad plate. Makes 4 servings. Double recipe for 8 servings.

MARINATED VEGETABLES

Good for barbecues . . . flavor blends with most foods

1 (14 oz.) can artichoke
hearts, drained and halved
1 (8 oz.) can sliced mushrooms,
drained
1 (7¼ oz.) can baby carrots,
drained
1 (2½ oz.) jar pimiento-stuffed
olives, drained

⅔ c. white vinegar
⅔ c. salad oil
2 tblsp. instant minced onion
1 tsp. Italian seasoning
1 tsp. salt
1 tsp. sugar
⅛ tsp. garlic powder
⅛ tsp. pepper

Combine artichokes, mushrooms, carrots and olives in bowl.

Combine vinegar, oil, instant minced onion, Italian seasoning, salt, sugar, garlic powder and pepper in small saucepan. Bring to a boil. Cool slightly, then pour over vegetables. Cover and refrigerate 12 hours, or overnight. Makes about 8 servings.

ARMENIAN RELISH

A tangy and colorful relish which complements most meats

1¼ c. cider vinegar
4 c. water
1 tblsp. salt
1 tblsp. caraway seeds
1 bunch green onions, tops
removed
1 large onion, thinly sliced
1 c. coarsely chopped cabbage

1 small unpeeled cucumber,
cubed
1 c. fresh whole mushrooms,
stems removed
3 carrots, pared and cut
in chunks
4 branches celery, cut in
chunks

Combine vinegar, water, salt and caraway seeds in saucepan and bring to a boil. Cool.

Combine onions, cabbage, cucumber, mushrooms, carrots and celery in large jar or crock. Cover with cooled liquid. Store in refrigerator at least 5 days. Drain and serve. Makes about 6 to 8 servings.

GREEK SALAD

Make it a main dish salad with crusty bread and fresh fruit

1 small onion, thinly sliced
1 head lettuce
1 c. cubed cooked potatoes
2 hard-cooked eggs, quartered
8 ripe olives

2 branches celery, thinly
  sliced
1 tsp. capers
Greek Salad Dressing (see
  Index)

Separate onion slices into rings.

Tear lettuce in bite-size pieces.

Combine onions with potatoes, eggs, olives, celery and capers. Add to lettuce in large bowl. Add Greek Salad Dressing (shake well before using) and toss to mix. Makes 4 servings. Double recipe for 8 servings.

SHRIMP AND COLESLAW SALAD

Tarragon accents shrimp pleasingly in this refreshing salad

½ c. mayonnaise
2 tblsp. lemon juice
1 tsp. dried tarragon leaves,
  finely crumbled
½ tsp. salt

1 c. finely shredded cabbage
1½ c. coarsely chopped cooked
  shrimp
Lettuce

Combine mayonnaise, lemon juice, tarragon and salt; mix thoroughly.

Place cabbage and shrimp in bowl; add mayonnaise mixture and toss together to blend. Serve on crisp lettuce. Makes 4 servings. Double recipe for 8 servings.

IMPERIAL CABBAGE SALAD

Freshly chopped chives make this cabbage salad so different

1½ c. boiling water
1 (3 oz.) pkg. lime flavor
  gelatin
¼ c. cold water
¼ c. Dill Wine Vinegar (see
  Index) or white wine vinegar

1 c. finely shredded cabbage
½ c. finely shredded carrot
¼ c. finely chopped green
  pepper
1 tblsp. very finely chopped
  fresh chives

Pour boiling water over gelatin; stir to dissolve. Add cold water and vinegar. Chill until slightly thickened.

Fold cabbage, carrot, green pepper and chives into gelatin. Pour into 1-qt. ring mold and chill until firm. Makes 4 to 6 servings.

TOSSED GREEN SALAD WITH HERBS

Herb French Dressing makes the tangy difference in this salad

1 head lettuce
2 tomatoes, chopped
1 unpeeled cucumber, chopped
4 small branches celery,
  chopped

6 to 8 radishes, very thinly
  sliced
Herb French Dressing (see
  Index)

Tear lettuce in bite-size pieces. Place in salad bowl and add tomatoes, cucumber, celery and radishes. Toss with Herb French Dressing (½ c.); serve at once. Makes 6 to 8 servings.

FROSTED TOMATOES

Garnish each individual serving with a sprig of fresh parsley

4 large ripe tomatoes
½ c. mayonnaise

¼ c. Herb Mustard (see Index)
Lettuce

Peel tomatoes, and chill until ready to serve.

Blend together mayonnaise and Herb Mustard; chill.

At serving time, place each tomato in a lettuce cup; cover tomato completely with mayonnaise-mustard mixture. Makes 4 servings. Double recipe for 8 servings.

BARBARA'S POTATO SALAD

If possible, chill potato salad at least 4 hours to give the variety of herbs a chance to contribute their best flavor blends

4 large potatoes
2 hard-cooked eggs, chopped
1 c. finely chopped celery
4 slices crisp-cooked bacon,
  crumbled
¼ c. pickle relish

½ c. mayonnaise
¼ c. Herb Mustard (see Index)
½ tsp. fresh or dried dill weed
1 tblsp. capers
¼ c. finely chopped fresh
  chives

Cook potatoes in jackets in boiling water. Peel and cube. Combine with remaining ingredients, and mix well. Chill. Makes 4 to 6 servings.

MARJORAM TUNA SALAD

This salad mixture is also delicious on open-faced sandwiches

1 c. chopped celery
2 tblsp. finely chopped onion
½ c. mayonnaise
¼ tsp. salt
½ tsp. ground marjoram

¼ tsp. pepper
2 (7 oz.) cans tuna, drained
  and flaked
Lettuce
Paprika

Combine celery, onion, mayonnaise, salt, marjoram, pepper and tuna; toss just enough to mix. Serve on lettuce; garnish with paprika. Makes 4 to 6 servings.

ORÉGANO TUNA SALAD

Substitute canned salmon for the tuna for a special luncheon

3 tblsp. instant minced onion	¼ tsp. pepper
3 tblsp. water	2 (7 oz.) cans tuna, drained
¾ c. mayonnaise	and flaked
½ tsp. dried orégano leaves, crumbled	1 c. finely chopped celery
	Lettuce

Combine instant minced onion with water; let stand 10 minutes. Stir occasionally. Combine onion with mayonnaise, orégano and pepper; mix well.

Place tuna and celery in large bowl. Add mayonnaise mixture and toss gently until blended. Serve on lettuce. Makes 6 servings.

BAKED CHICKEN SALAD

You'll receive many compliments when you serve this hot salad

2½ c. cubed cooked chicken	1 c. mayonnaise
½ c. finely chopped celery	½ c. chicken broth
¾ c. finely chopped green pepper	½ tsp. Salad Herbs (see Index)
½ c. slivered almonds	1 tsp. salt
2 hard-cooked eggs, chopped	½ tsp. pepper
	½ c. shredded Cheddar cheese

Combine chicken, celery, green pepper, almonds, eggs, mayonnaise, broth, Salad Herbs, salt and pepper. Mix together well. Spoon into 1½-qt. casserole. Sprinkle cheese over top.

Bake in moderate oven (375°) about 30 minutes, or until bubbling and golden brown on top. Makes 6 servings.

Superb Sauces and Dressings

The dictionary defines a sauce as "an appetizing accompaniment to food; a preparation to give zest to a dish." What more can we ask of sauces and dressings than this? We can, however, add zest to our sauces and dressings with just the right herb. The right sauce on the right dish saves an otherwise flat or dull menu.

You'll find sauces and dressings for fruits, vegetables, salads, fish, meat, casseroles and desserts in this chapter, all of them easy to prepare.

Vegetables become monotonous fixed the same old way, so try adding cheese sauce to asparagus, cauliflower, broccoli or Brussels sprouts. Do your "regular boarders" grow listless at the sight of green beans? Dress them up with an herb sauce. Even spinach and other greens take on a new personality with the addition of a sauce.

Butter sauces, cream sauces, all sorts of sauces are improved with herbs. And don't forget that Herb Mustard (see Index) makes a new sauce out of an old one—1 tablespoon for 4 servings is a general rule, unless you like more zip. Herb French Dressing (see Index) added to your own recipes can make a distinctive difference.

Fish particularly seems to need a sauce for zest. Basil, chives, dill, parsley and tarragon are all herbs you can stir into a fish sauce to add a special taste. And you don't have to look for new recipes—try your own recipes plus an herb for flavor, and see what luscious combinations you can discover.

You'll notice that the sauce recipes call for cornstarch instead of flour as a thickener. That's because cornstarch mixes more easily, to make a creamier, lump-free sauce. Also, cornstarch gives up its "pasty" taste more readily than flour.

MINTED FRUIT SAUCE

Both fresh and canned fruit are good with this minted sauce

1 tsp. lemon juice	1 c. plain yogurt
¾ tsp. mint flakes, crumbled	3 tblsp. brown sugar
½ tsp. grated lemon peel	

Mix lemon juice with mint flakes and lemon peel. Let stand 2 minutes.

In small bowl blend yogurt with brown sugar. Add mint mixture and mix well. Refrigerate at least 1 hour. Makes 1 cup.

WHIPPED CREAM DRESSING

A delicate mint-flavored dressing for any fresh fruit salad

2 tblsp. mint jelly	2 tblsp. mayonnaise
1 tblsp. lemon juice	½ c. heavy cream, whipped

Mash jelly with a fork. Add lemon juice and mayonnaise; mix thoroughly. Fold in whipped cream. Makes 1 cup.

SOUR CREAM DRESSING (FOR FRUIT)

Combine drained, canned peaches and pears for an elegant salad

1 c. dairy sour cream	1 tblsp. confectioners sugar
2 tblsp. milk	¼ tsp. salt
1 tsp. lemon juice	¼ tsp. aniseeds

Combine all ingredients and mix well. Chill until ready to serve. Makes 1¼ cups.

MARSHMALLOW MINT SAUCE

Try this for a chocolate marshmallow mint sundae

¼ c. boiling water	16 to 20 large marshmallows
4 tblsp. fresh mint leaves, crushed	1 or 2 drops green food coloring

Pour boiling water over mint leaves. Steep for about 30 minutes. Strain liquid. Pour liquid back in saucepan and bring to a boil. Add marshmallows; stir constantly over low heat until marshmallows have melted and mixture is smooth. Add green food coloring. Chill. Makes 1½ cups.

TARRAGON PICKLE SAUCE

A great accompaniment to fish dishes as well as salads

½ c. sweet pickle relish
¼ c. olive oil or salad oil
¾ tsp. dried tarragon leaves, crumbled

1 tsp. instant minced onion
¼ tsp. garlic powder
2 tblsp. white vinegar
1 tblsp. lemon juice

Combine all ingredients and blend well. Cover and refrigerate 1 hour or longer. Stir thoroughly just before serving. Makes about 1 cup.

ENGLISH CHEESE SAUCE

Also good served over toast and garnished with a tomato slice

1½ c. milk
2 tblsp. cornstarch
Water

1 c. grated sharp process cheese
1 tsp. curry powder

Scald milk in double boiler.

Mix cornstarch with a little water to make a smooth paste; add to milk in saucepan and cook over low heat, stirring constantly, until mixture thickens. Add cheese and curry powder; continue to stir until cheese is melted and mixture is smooth. Makes about 2 cups.

PARMESAN CHEESE SAUCE

Herb Mustard is the secret . . . so good over hot vegetables

2 tblsp. cornstarch
1½ c. milk
2 tblsp. sherry

2 tblsp. Herb Mustard (see Index)
½ c. grated Parmesan cheese

Mix cornstarch with a little milk to make a smooth paste. Combine with remaining milk in saucepan and cook over low heat until thickened, stirring constantly. Add sherry, Herb Mustard and cheese. Simmer about 10 minutes, stirring constantly, until cheese is melted and sauce is smooth. Makes 1⅔ cups.

CREAM CHEESE/CHIVES DRESSING

Doubles as a salad dressing and a sauce for baked potatoes

1 (3 oz.) pkg. cream cheese	¼ c. finely chopped fresh
¼ c. light cream	chives

Soften cream cheese at room temperature, then whip in cream and chives. Makes about ¾ cup.

DILL SAUCE

Especially good served with potatoes, cabbage or broiled fish

¼ c. butter or regular margarine	1 tsp. Herb Salt (see Index)
2 tblsp. cornstarch	¾ tsp. dried dill weed
2 c. milk	

Melt butter in saucepan. Add cornstarch and stir to blend. Add milk; cook, stirring constantly, until thick and smooth. Add Herb Salt and dill weed; stir to mix. Serve hot. Makes 2¼ cups.

PARSLEY SAUCE

Perfect cream sauce for all vegetables and croquettes

2 tblsp. butter or regular margarine	½ tsp. salt
2 tblsp. cornstarch	½ c. finely chopped fresh parsley
1½ c. milk	

Melt butter in saucepan; remove from heat and blend in cornstarch to make a smooth paste. Gradually blend in milk. Return to heat, add salt and cook, stirring constantly, until mixture thickens and makes a smooth sauce. Add chopped parsley and heat through. Makes about 1½ cups.

THYME BUTTER

Keep on hand in the refrigerator to serve on meat or fish

1 c. softened butter or regular margarine
¼ tsp. ground thyme

Combine butter and thyme; blend well. Makes 1 cup.

NOTE: Any other favorite herb can be substituted for thyme.

SPECIAL ASPIC DRESSING

Always a favorite, especially over shimmering aspic squares

1 (3 oz.) pkg. cream cheese   2 tblsp. light cream
1 tblsp. lemon juice   1 tsp. Salad Herbs (see Index)

Let cream cheese stand at room temperature to soften, then combine with lemon juice, cream and Salad Herbs. Whip until smooth and blended. Makes about ⅔ cup.

GREEK SALAD DRESSING

Adds zest to any green salad. Try it on the Greek Salad too

2 tblsp. salad oil   1 tsp. salt
2 tblsp. olive oil   1 tsp. sugar
2 tblsp. cider vinegar   1 tsp. dry mustard
1 tsp. paprika

Combine all ingredients in small jar; shake to mix well. Chill at least 1 hour. Shake again before serving. Keeps several days. Makes about ½ cup.

SOUR CREAM DRESSING (FOR VEGETABLES)

This sour cream dressing is good over hot or cold vegetables

1 egg
1 c. dairy sour cream
1 tblsp. Dill Wine Vinegar (see Index) or white wine vinegar

2 tblsp. honey
½ tsp. salt
1 tblsp. Herb Mustard (see Index)

Beat egg thoroughly in small bowl of electric mixer. Beat in sour cream. Add vinegar, honey, salt and Herb Mustard; beat until smooth and velvety. Makes 1½ cups.

ITALIAN SALAD DRESSING

Double this dressing recipe to keep on hand for everyday use

¾ c. salad oil or olive oil
6 tblsp. wine vinegar
½ tsp. garlic powder
¼ tsp. dried orégano leaves, crumbled

½ tsp. dried basil leaves, crumbled
½ tsp. salt
½ tsp. pepper
¼ tsp. sugar

Combine all ingredients. Let stand at least 1 hour.
Beat salad dressing with a rotary beater. Use to serve over mixed salad greens. Makes 1 cup.

HERB FRENCH DRESSING

You'll never use plain French dressing again after trying this

1 (8 oz.) bottle French dressing
1 tblsp. lemon juice
1 tsp. dried tarragon leaves, crumbled

1 tsp. parsley flakes, crumbled
1 tsp. dried basil leaves, crumbled
½ tsp. dried dill weed
¼ tsp. celery salt

Pour French dressing into a quart jar. Add lemon juice, tarragon, parsley, basil, dill and celery salt. Cover and shake thoroughly. Refrigerate for a week for herbs to flavor the dressing. Makes 1 cup.

Sandwiches and Special Spreads

If you have school lunch boxes to pack, you're probably looking for a change from peanut butter and tuna fish. Imagination and a slight urge to gamble will help you.

You can lean heavily on packaged cream cheese, for it will serve as a base for many combinations. It goes well with fish, ground meats, grated vegetables, and even mashed fruits and jellies.

The little cans of tuna, shrimp, crab, salmon, olive butter and deviled ham all mix well with nuts, cheese, herbs and shredded vegetables for variety. Hard-cooked eggs, too, can be added to all these.

Herb Vinegar and Herb Mustard make excellent thinners for sandwich fillings or for the mayonnaise used with sandwiches. Herb Butter makes a perfect base for any type of sandwich—for the lunch box, the bridge party, the hot late-supper sandwich. (See Index for the above herb recipes.)

Basil, sage, thyme, savory and parsley all go well with meat fillings. Dill, marjoram, orégano, burnet and parsley unite happily with vegetable fillings. Basil, chives, tarragon, dill and parsley are good with egg and cheese fillings.

Here's a little trick I used with my children which might be helpful for you. If they didn't happen to like an herb combination I had used with meat or fish or cheese, I would stop short after their protest and say, "Oh, yes, I forgot—you're not quite *old* enough yet to enjoy that flavor." It always worked!

MEXICAN SANDWICHES

Potato chips and crisp dill pickles are great with these buns

1 lb. ground beef	¼ tsp. dried orégano leaves,
1 c. finely chopped onion	finely crumbled
1 tsp. chili powder	6 frankfurter buns, split
¼ tsp. dried basil leaves, finely	2 tblsp. Herb Butter (see
crumbled	Index)

In heavy skillet, brown ground beef with onion, breaking up with a fork to separate meat. Pour off fat. Add chili powder, basil and orégano, mixing well. Cook until meat is done, about 10 minutes.

Spread rolls with Herb Butter; spoon meat mixture into rolls. Fasten with wooden picks, if necessary. Place filled rolls on baking sheet; bake in moderate oven (375°) 5 to 10 minutes, or until toasted. Makes 6 sandwiches.

BAKED CHICKEN/HAM SANDWICHES

Also good with different cooked meats, such as pork or beef

1 c. finely chopped cooked	1 tsp. salt
chicken	2 tblsp. chopped ripe olives
1 c. finely chopped cooked ham	¼ c. chopped celery
½ c. shredded sharp process	½ c. mayonnaise
cheese	12 slices white bread
½ tsp. dried tarragon leaves,	¼ c. milk
finely crumbled	3 eggs, well beaten

Mix chicken, ham, cheese, tarragon, salt, olives and celery with mayonnaise (add a little more mayonnaise if mixture seems dry). Spread mixture on 6 slices bread; top with remaining bread.

Mix milk with beaten eggs. Using two forks or wide spatulas, carefully dip both sides of each sandwich in egg-milk mixture; wrap in plastic wrap or foil. Refrigerate overnight.

When ready to cook, unwrap sandwiches and place on buttered baking sheet. Bake in hot oven (400°) about 20 minutes, or until crisp and brown. Makes 6 sandwiches.

SOUTHERN HAM SANDWICHES

So simple to make . . . uses English muffins instead of bread

4 English muffins, split
Herb Butter (see Index)
8 slices baked ham

8 slices sharp process cheese
8 tomato slices

Spread each muffin half with Herb Butter. Place a slice of ham and cheese on each. Top with a tomato slice. Place in hot oven (400°) about 10 minutes, or until muffins are crisp and cheese melted. Makes 8 open-face sandwiches.

SALMON SANDWICH SPREAD

Spread on party rye slices to make elegant hors d'oeuvres

1 (1 lb.) can salmon
¼ c. finely chopped celery
1 tblsp. finely chopped fresh
  parsley
1 tblsp. lemon juice

1 tblsp. Tarragon Wine Vinegar
  (see Index) or red wine
  vinegar
½ c. mayonnaise

Drain and flake salmon, removing bones and skin. Combine with celery, parsley, lemon juice, vinegar and mayonnaise; blend well. Chill. Makes 2 cups.

TEA SANDWICH SPREAD

Make these tea sandwiches the night before and refrigerate

4 hard-cooked eggs, finely
  chopped
8 pimiento-stuffed olives,
  chopped

1 tblsp. Herb Mustard (see
  Index)
¼ c. mayonnaise

Combine eggs, olives, Herb Mustard and mayonnaise. Mash together until well blended. Chill. Makes about 1¼ cups.

EGG/CREAM CHEESE SPREAD

The herbs make all the difference in this smooth, creamy spread

1 (3 oz.) pkg. cream cheese
4 hard-cooked eggs, finely
  chopped

3 tblsp. Herb French Dressing
  (see Index)
1 tsp. Salad Herbs (see Index)

Soften cream cheese at room temperature, then combine with eggs, Herb French Dressing and Salad Herbs. Blend well, and chill. Makes about 1¼ cups.

NOTE: You can substitute regular French dressing for Herb French Dressing, but use 1 tblsp. instead of 1 tsp. Salad Herbs.

DEVILED EGG SPREAD

Deviled egg lovers will like this tasty sandwich spread

4 hard-cooked eggs, chopped
½ c. finely chopped celery
2 tblsp. Herb Mustard (see
  Index)
¼ tsp. salt

¼ tsp. pepper
¼ tsp. dried basil leaves, finely
  crumbled
2 tblsp. mayonnaise

Combine eggs, celery, Herb Mustard, salt, pepper, basil and mayonnaise; blend well. Chill. Makes 2 cups.

DEVILED TUNA SPREAD

Parsley and curry powder add flavor, the nuts add crunchiness

1 (13 oz.) can water-pack tuna,
  drained and flaked
2 tblsp. pickle relish
¼ c. finely chopped walnuts

1 tblsp. parsley flakes, finely
  crumbled
½ tsp. curry powder
½ c. mayonnaise

Mix tuna with pickle relish. Add walnuts, parsley and curry powder; mix together. Add mayonnaise and blend thoroughly. Makes about 2½ cups, enough filling for 6 to 8 sandwiches.

HOMEMADE PIMIENTO CHEESE

Spread on crackers and garnish with chopped fresh parsley

1 (4 oz.) jar pimientos   1 tsp. parsley flakes
1 lb. sharp process cheese,
  shredded

Drain pimientos, reserving liquid. Place pimiento liquid in blender first; add cheese, a little at a time, with blender set at lowest speed. Blend until smooth and creamy. Add parsley, then pimientos. Blend 2 or 3 seconds more. Pack in covered container. Makes 1½ cups.

Delightful Desserts

You didn't think that herbs could be used in desserts? You're in for a surprise. Some of them can really give a lift to an ordinary dessert and produce a very different and delicious ending to a meal.

Anise and caraway seeds are delicious in cookies. This chapter features a delicate crisp macaroon with a gentle flavoring of aniseeds and a meringue kiss with a hint of mint flavoring. Do try the Lemon/Caraway Cookies—the dough can be refrigerated and then thinly sliced when you're ready to bake a batch of cookies.

You will like the whisper of coriander in the Easy Pecan Pie and the unusual but interesting flavor of rosemary in the Special Mincemeat Tarts.

The rich Red Raspberry Mousse and the Frozen Chocolate Mint Charlotte have a subtle undertone of mint . . . both of these "elegants" are perfect to serve special guests.

On a blustery winter evening, the family will welcome a serving of Quick Peach Cobbler scented with anise-flavored syrup or a dish of Spiced Mixed Fruit that has just a touch of rosemary in the spicy syrup.

In addition to the recipes in this chapter, there are many quick desserts that can be made with a hint of rosemary, mint, caraway or coriander. Add a tiny pinch of coriander in pie crust or stir a spoonful of anise-flavored syrup into a batch of creamy vanilla pudding. Or, trickle mint-flavored syrup over lemon sherbet for a refreshing grand finale.

EASY MACAROONS

These crisp cookies have the distinct flavor of aniseeds; you may want to substitute sesame seeds for the anise

2 egg whites	1 tsp. almond extract
½ c. sugar	1 tsp. aniseeds
¼ tsp. salt	2 c. oven-toasted rice cereal

Beat egg whites until stiff. Beat in sugar and salt. Fold in almond extract, aniseeds and cereal. Drop by teaspoonfuls 2″ apart onto greased baking sheet.

Bake in very slow oven (250°) 25 minutes for crisp cookies, 15 minutes for softer ones. Remove from baking sheet and cool on racks. Makes 3 dozen.

NUT KISSES

Meringue cookies rich with almonds and just a hint of mint

¼ tsp. salt	½ tsp. vanilla
2 egg whites	¼ tsp. peppermint extract
½ c. sugar	½ c. chopped toasted almonds

Add salt to egg whites and beat until stiff. Gradually add sugar, beating constantly. Continue beating until stiff glossy peaks form.

Fold in vanilla, peppermint extract and almonds. Drop by teaspoonfuls 2″ apart onto greased baking sheet.

Bake in slow oven (300°) 30 minutes, or until lightly browned. Remove from baking sheet and cool on racks. Makes 2 dozen.

NOTE: You can substitute ¼ tsp. almond extract for the peppermint, if you like.

SCOTCH RIDGE PECAN STICKS

A favorite snack—these rich sesame cookies and glasses of milk

¼ c. shortening
1 c. brown sugar, firmly
  packed
1 egg
1 c. sifted cake flour

1 tsp. baking powder
¼ tsp. salt
1 c. pecan pieces
Sesame seeds

Cream together shortening, sugar and egg.

Sift together flour, baking powder and salt. Add to creamed mixture, mixing well. Stir in nuts. Spread evenly in waxed paper-lined 8″ square pan. Sprinkle with sesame seeds.

Bake in moderate oven (350°) 15 minutes, or until light brown. Set pan on rack. When cool, cut in 2½ ✕ ¾″ sticks. Makes 2 dozen.

LEMON/CARAWAY COOKIES

Keep rolls of dough in refrigerator to bake on short notice

1 egg
1 c. sugar
2½ c. sifted flour
½ tsp. baking soda

½ tsp. salt
2 tblsp. lemon juice
½ c. shortening
1 tsp. caraway seeds

Beat egg. Gradually beat in sugar, creaming well.

Sift together flour, soda and salt.

Add lemon juice, shortening, caraway seeds and sifted dry ingredients to creamed mixture, blending well. Shape into rolls about 2″ in diameter; wrap in foil or waxed paper and chill in refrigerator.

Cut rolls in thin slices; place about 1″ apart on ungreased baking sheet.

Bake in hot oven (400°) 8 minutes, or until light brown. Remove from baking sheet and cool on racks. Makes 3½ dozen.

SWEDISH BALLS

These attractive, buttery cookies are lovely with lime sherbet

1 c. butter or regular margarine	1 tsp. aniseeds
½ c. sugar	1 c. chopped pecans or walnuts
¼ tsp. salt	2 c. unsifted flour
1 tsp. vanilla	Confectioners sugar

Cream together butter and sugar. Add salt, vanilla, aniseeds and nuts. Knead in flour with your hands (this will be a dry mixture). When thoroughly mixed, roll into balls the size of a walnut. Place about 1″ apart on ungreased baking sheet.

Bake in moderate oven (350°) 25 minutes, or until lightly browned. Remove cookies from baking sheet and roll in confectioners sugar while still warm. Cool on racks. Makes about 3 dozen.

EASY PECAN PIE

Top wedges of this delicious pecan pie with soft whipped cream

Pastry for 1-crust pie	¼ c. butter or regular
½ c. sugar	margarine
1 c. light corn syrup	¼ tsp. ground coriander
3 eggs, well beaten	1 c. pecan halves
1 tsp. vanilla	

Prepare an unbaked 8″ pie shell.

Combine sugar and corn syrup in top of double boiler over medium heat. Heat until sugar dissolves. Gradually add eggs, stirring constantly. Add vanilla, butter and coriander, and cook, continuing to stir, until mixture thickens slightly. Remove from heat. Stir in pecans; pour into pastry-lined pie pan.

Bake in hot oven (400°) 15 minutes; reduce heat to moderate (350°) and bake 20 minutes longer. Cool. Makes 8 servings.

SPECIAL MINCEMEAT TARTS

Make these tarts ahead and freeze for the busy holiday season

Pastry for 2-crust pie
2 c. prepared mincemeat
¼ c. sweet apple cider

¼ tsp. dried rosemary leaves,
    finely crumbled
Hard sauce or whipped cream

Prepare pastry and roll out very thin. Cut in eight 6″ squares. Line muffin-pan cups with pastry squares, letting corners extend over top.

Mix mincemeat with cider and rosemary. Place about ⅓ c. mixture in each pastry-lined muffin-pan cup. Fold corners of pastry over top. Cut vents.

Bake in hot oven (425°) 30 minutes. Serve warm, topped with hard sauce or whipped cream. Makes 8 tarts.

ANGEL PIE

A great make-ahead dessert that is refrigerated until served

1 c. chocolate cookie crumbs
2 tblsp. melted butter or regular
    margarine
1 envelope unflavored gelatin
¼ c. cold water
¼ c. boiling water

1 tsp. vanilla
¼ tsp. aniseeds
3 egg whites
½ c. sugar
1 c. heavy cream, whipped

Combine cookie crumbs and melted butter; blend well. Set aside 1 tblsp. crumb mixture for garnish. Press remaining crumbs into 9″ pie pan; chill until firm.

Soften gelatin in cold water. Add boiling water, vanilla and aniseeds; stir to dissolve gelatin.

Beat egg whites until soft peaks form; add sugar, 1 tblsp. at a time, beating well after each addition. Beat until stiff peaks form. Fold in gelatin, then fold in whipped cream. Refrigerate just until mixture starts to set, then spoon into crumb crust. Sprinkle reserved crumbs over top; chill until set. Makes 6 to 8 servings.

RED RASPBERRY MOUSSE

Your guests will ask for seconds when you serve this

2 (3 oz.) pkgs. raspberry flavor gelatin
2 c. boiling water
2 (10 oz.) pkgs. frozen red raspberries, partially thawed
1 pt. heavy cream

⅛ tsp. peppermint extract
12 ladyfingers, split lengthwise
Whipped cream
Fresh mint leaves

Dissolve gelatin in boiling water; stir to dissolve. Add raspberries, stir until completely thawed. Chill mixture until thick and very syrupy.

Whip cream with peppermint extract until soft peaks form. Gently fold whipped cream into gelatin mixture. Chill 10 minutes in refrigerator.

Line an 8″ spring-form pan with ladyfingers, rounded side out. Pour mixture into pan. Chill until set. Decorate top of dessert with puffs of whipped cream and mint leaves. Makes 10 servings.

FROZEN CHOCOLATE MINT CHARLOTTE

This teams two all-time favorites—chocolate and mint. Especially good served with Marshmallow Mint Sauce (see Index)

2 tblsp. fresh or dried mint leaves
2 tblsp. boiling water

1 c. heavy cream
1 (6½ oz.) pkg. chocolate frosting mix

Add mint to boiling water and steep about 20 minutes.

Whip cream until stiff. Carefully fold in frosting mix a little at a time.

Strain mint. Fold liquid into chocolate mixture. Pour into refrigerator tray and freeze until firm. Makes 4 to 6 servings.

QUICK PEACH COBBLER

It's the anise-flavored syrup poured over the peaches before baking that makes this cobbler taste so good

1 (1 lb. 13 oz.) can sliced peaches	¼ tsp. aniseeds
	1 tblsp. lemon juice
¼ c. sugar	1 c. all-purpose buttermilk
⅛ tsp. salt	biscuit mix
1 tblsp. cornstarch	¼ c. milk

Drain peaches, reserving 1 c. syrup. Place peach slices in 8" square baking pan.

Combine sugar, salt, cornstarch and aniseeds. Gradually add reserved peach syrup and lemon juice, blending to make a smooth mixture. Pour over peaches.

Combine biscuit mix and milk; mix well. On well-floured board, roll out pastry to ¼" thickness. Cut in strips; arrange strips in crisscross (lattice) fashion over top of peaches; trim off excess pastry and press strips firmly against inside of pan.

Bake in very hot oven (450°) 30 minutes, or until crust is brown. Makes 4 to 6 servings.

SPICED MIXED FRUIT

Serve this light dessert with cookies or wedges of cheese

1 c. sugar	2 (8 oz.) cans pineapple chunks, drained, or 2 c. fresh pineapple chunks
¾ c. water	
¼ tsp. dried rosemary leaves, crushed	
	2 c. sliced apples
2 (2") sticks cinnamon	4 c. orange sections
¼ tsp. whole cloves	1 tblsp. lemon juice

Combine sugar, water, rosemary, cinnamon and cloves in saucepan. Bring to a boil; reduce heat and simmer 10 minutes. Remove from heat and cool; strain.

In mixing bowl combine pineapple, apples, orange sections and lemon juice. Pour strained syrup over fruit and mix well. Chill. To serve, spoon into sherbet glasses. Makes 12 servings.

Homemade Herb Jellies

I'm sure you've enjoyed mint jelly with pork or lamb—it's easily available in markets. But have you ever thought about flavoring fruit jellies with other herbs like rosemary, sage or marjoram? You'll make some elegant meat accompaniments if you experiment with the easy recipes in this chapter—Marjoram/ Lemon Jelly, Grape and Sage Jelly or Spiced Ruby Cranberry Jelly. And some of them may be used in or on desserts, with salads and hot breads or rolls.

If you have the perfect recipe for the perfect jelly, use it and simply add an herb for additional flavor. Or sample our 7 easy recipes, all quick to make, lovely to look at, delicious to eat.

The best way to get herb flavor into a jelly is to make a bag for the herbs. Cut cheesecloth or fine net into 6-inch squares, place either fresh or dried herbs in the center of the square, draw up the corners and tie tightly with thread or string. Drop this bag into the fruit juice and allow to simmer for 20 minutes. Remove the bag, and go on with your jelly-making.

After you have sampled these tasty jellies, you'll want to share them with your friends. See the Herbs Make Glamorous Gifts section for suggestions on how to gift-package herb jellies for Christmas and other special occasions.

SPICED GRAPE JELLY

So good on hot, buttered corn muffins or piping hot popovers

2 c. grape juice	¼ tsp. whole cloves
1 c. water	1 pkg. powdered fruit pectin
½ tsp. dried rosemary leaves, crushed	3½ c. sugar

Pour juice and water into large kettle. Add rosemary and cloves, tied in clean, thin white cloth. Stir in pectin. Place over high heat and stir until mixture comes to a full rolling boil. Add sugar at once; mix well. Bring to a full rolling boil again. Boil 1 minute, stirring constantly.

Remove from heat, and discard rosemary and cloves; skim. Pour into hot glasses or jars. Cover with paraffin at once or adjust lids on jars and process in boiling water bath (212°) 5 minutes. Remove from canner and complete seals unless closures are self-sealing type. Makes 3 half pints.

CIDER/SAGE JELLY

A perfect hostess gift tied with a pretty colored ribbon

1 (1 qt.) bottle or can apple juice or fresh cider	1 pkg. powdered fruit pectin
	2 tblsp. dried sage leaves
3 drops green food color	5 c. sugar

Combine apple juice, food color, pectin and sage, tied in clean, thin white cloth, in large saucepan. Place over high heat and stir until liquid comes to a hard boil.

At once stir in sugar; bring to a full rolling boil. Boil hard, stirring constantly, 3 to 5 minutes to jellying stage (219 to 221° on candy thermometer), or until two drops run together and sheet off a metal spoon.

Remove from heat and discard sage; skim. Pour into hot glasses or jars. Cover with paraffin at once or adjust lids on jars and process in boiling water bath (212°) 5 minutes. Remove from canner and complete seals unless closures are self-sealing type. Makes 8 half pints.

SPICED RUBY CRANBERRY JELLY

The hint of rosemary in this clear red jelly makes it special

1 pkg. powdered fruit pectin	½ tsp. dried rosemary leaves
1½ c. ruby port	3 c. sugar
½ c. cranberry juice cocktail	

Mix together pectin, port and cranberry juice cocktail in saucepan; stir until pectin dissolves. Add rosemary, tied in clean, thin white cloth.

Place over high heat and cook, stirring constantly, until mixture comes to a full rolling boil. Add sugar all at once and return to a full boil. Boil 1 minute, stirring constantly.

Remove from heat and discard rosemary; skim. Pour into hot glasses or jars. Cover with paraffin at once or adjust lids on jars and process in boiling water bath (212°) 5 minutes. Remove from canner and complete seals unless closures are self-sealing type. Makes about 6 half pints.

APPLE MINT JELLY

Try with roast lamb . . . you'll never want plain mint jelly again

2 c. canned or bottled apple juice	3½ c. sugar
	½ c. liquid fruit pectin
2 tblsp. fresh mint or mint flakes	3 or 4 drops green food color

Place apple juice in 3-qt. saucepan. Add mint, tied in clean, thin white cloth; simmer 20 minutes. Remove mint.

Measure juice; add more apple juice if necessary to make 2 c. Add sugar to apple juice and bring to a full rolling boil. Add pectin and enough food color to tint a brilliant green; bring to a boil again, and boil 30 seconds.

Remove from heat; skim. Pour into hot glasses or jars. Cover with paraffin at once or adjust lids on jars and process in boiling water bath (212°) 5 minutes. Remove from canner and complete seals unless closures are self-sealing type. Makes 4 half pints.

CIDER AND ROSEMARY JELLY

Make up several batches of this jelly . . . everyone will like it

2 c. sweet apple cider	3½ c. sugar
2 tblsp. fresh rosemary leaves	½ c. liquid fruit pectin

Pour cider into 3-qt. saucepan. Add rosemary leaves, tied in clean, thin white cloth; simmer 20 minutes. Remove rosemary.

Measure juice; add more cider if necessary to make 2 c. Add sugar and bring to a full rolling boil. Add pectin; bring to a boil again and boil 30 seconds.

Remove from heat; skim. Pour into hot glasses or jars. Cover with paraffin at once or adjust lids on jars and process in boiling water bath (212°) 5 minutes. Remove from canner and complete seals unless closures are self-sealing type. Makes 4 half pints.

MARJORAM/LEMON JELLY

Spoon into an attractive glass dish, serve with a basket of hot rolls and grilled or broiled steaks or chops

2 c. bottled or fresh lemon juice	4 c. sugar
2 tblsp. fresh or dried marjoram leaves	½ c. liquid fruit pectin

Pour lemon juice into 3-qt. saucepan. Add marjoram leaves, tied in clean, thin white cloth; simmer 20 minutes. Remove marjoram.

Measure juice; add more lemon juice if necessary to make 2 c. Add sugar and bring to a full rolling boil. Add pectin; bring to a boil again and boil 30 seconds.

Remove from heat; skim. Pour into hot glasses or jars. Cover with paraffin at once or adjust lids on jars and process in boiling water bath (212°) 5 minutes. Remove from canner and complete seals unless closures are self-sealing type. Makes about 4 half pints.

GRAPE AND SAGE JELLY

Serve on hot biscuits with chicken, roast pork or game

2 tblsp. fresh or dried sage leaves	3½ c. sugar
2 c. bottled grape juice	½ c. liquid fruit pectin

Tie sage in clean thin white cloth; add to grape juice in 3-qt. saucepan and simmer about 20 minutes. Remove sage. Add sugar to grape juice and bring to a full rolling boil. Stir in pectin and boil 30 seconds.

Remove from heat. Skim. Pour into hot glasses or jars. Cover with paraffin at once or adjust lids on jars and process in boiling water bath (212°) 5 minutes. Remove from canner and complete seals unless closures are self-sealing type. Makes about 4 half pints.

PART II

How to Grow Your Own Herbs

Growing herbs outside your kitchen door will daily reward your senses. The plants are relatively small, easy to tuck in among your flowers, attractive in a small herb bed or more extensive herb garden (see Planning and Designing Your Herb Garden). As you weed or pick flowers, pinch off a leaf of lemon balm or sweet basil and taste it, or crush it in your palm and sniff—pure pleasure!

With only minimal care, you can enjoy fresh herbs all summer long in your cooking—and on into winter too. A special section explains how to grow herbs indoors, on a window sill or under fluorescent lights. When bringing your outdoor plants indoors for the winter, be sure to allow for a transition period; dig up the plant and place it into a pot with plenty of its own soil, then leave it outside for two weeks until it adjusts to the potting.

You'll find an easy way to dry and store your summer harvest for winter use, and decorative ideas for uniquely personalized gifts in this section.

Whether your garden is indoors or out, please don't use weed killers or pesticides around your herbs! And don't laugh at this next statement: It definitely has been proven that plants that are *loved* and *talked to* will thrive better than those that are ignored. Richard Martin, writing in the *Wall Street Journal,* reported that Backster Research Associates had discovered that plants wilt and wither if scolded or threatened! So give praise and encouragement to your herb garden; plants need your tender, loving care.

Planning and Designing Your Herb Garden

Like any other project, the success of your herb garden depends upon careful planning. It's important first of all to make a plan on paper, showing a scale model of your proposed garden and where you would like your herbs to be situated. Determining factors for where you will place the herbs are how much area is to be covered, the general environmental conditions (sun or shade, dry or moist, etc.), the characteristics of your herbs (foliage, height, etc.) and your taste in style—whether formal or informal.

The following three designs are basic garden shapes. You can use them as they are illustrated—or use them as a springboard for your own innovations.

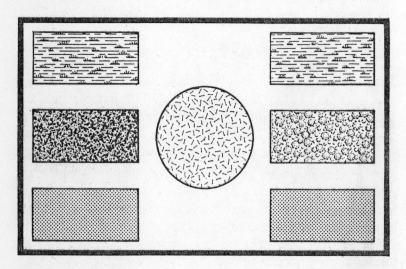

The Formal Garden

This garden design is as flexible as it is charming. It may have 6, 8, or as many little beds as you want and have room for. The beds are usually about 3' long by 2' wide, but can be any size—just make them rectangular and of uniform dimension. Cover the center path with flagstone, fine gravel, or creeping thyme and the paths between the beds with fine wood chips (they keep down the weeds). Or plant these paths with creeping thyme, too, for an especially lovely effect. The paths are just wide enough to permit the gardener to walk through the beds to pick herbs or pull an occasional weed. The circle in the center represents a center of interest—sun dial, bird bath, statue or fountain. The best herbs for these little beds are the low-growing, fragrant, old-fashioned herbs: English lavender, clove pinks, rosemary, lemon balm, sweet woodruff, heliotrope, pineapple mint, apple mint and the scented geraniums. Violets, lily of the valley, nasturtiums, cornflowers, English daisies, and santolina fit well and are attractive also. Beds may be bordered with parsley, ajuga or one of the variegated thymes such as golden, silver or lemon.

The Ladder Garden

This is an ideal plan for a purely culinary garden, since it is designed to follow a backyard path, or be planted along the side or back of the house nearest the kitchen door. You could imbed an actual ladder in the earth to define the beds, or outline them with wooden slats, bricks or small rocks. At the most, the garden should be only 3 or 4' wide so you can weed and pick from either side; if you place it against the house, beds should be a comfortable arm's reach.

The best culinary herbs for this garden are: Burnet, chives, thyme, savory, rosemary, basil, parsley, marjoram, orégano, French tarragon and sage.

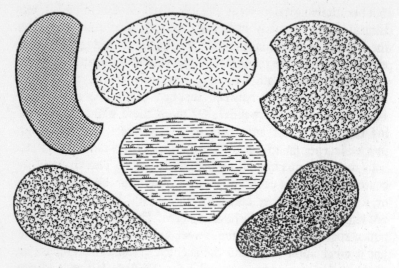

The Free-Form Garden

This modern type of herb garden is rapidly growing in popularity. It may contain as many beds as you have room for, and the beds may be any shape. To give a free-form garden a sense of order, the paths between should be neatly paved with fine gravel or wood chips.

Contrast is important in this type of herb garden. Select the herbs which will give you the most variety in flower colors, colors of foliage, foliage texture and height. Good herbs for the free-form garden include the variegated thymes—lemon, golden, silver and English. You'll like the effect of the silver of santolina against the shiny green of germander and the contrasts when you plant calendula, primrose, rue and southernwood together. Also interesting are the rough leaves of lemon balm against the piny spiked leaves of rosemary and lavender.

Once you have decided upon the area size of the garden and its arrangement, the next step is to prepare the soil. Perhaps you want to have the soil tested before beginning work, to be sure it is neither too sweet nor too acid. You can call your local office of the U. S. Department of Agriculture for information

about soil testing; you can get in touch with your County Agri-
cultural Agent; you can take a soil sample to almost any place
where fertilizer is sold and have the soil analyzed; or you can
purchase a soil-testing kit at most any seed store or from a landscape gardener and do the testing yourself.

Now you are ready to prepare the ground. If your area is to be
a small one (12×12'), this can be done by spading up the soil
to a depth of 6 to 8", breaking up clods or lumps, removing
all rocks larger than pebbles, and raking the whole area smooth
and level. If you plan a larger garden, you may want to buy
or rent a small riding garden tractor, or hire someone with a
large tractor to come in and plow, disk and harrow.

What is the best soil mix? Most of the herbs in the following
lists will grow well in poor soil. What is "poor soil?" It is soil
that is more than half sand; soil containing a small amount of
gravel; soil which contains no mulch; a heavy clay; soil with a
low lime content. But a good loam, with some sand, and mulch,
well drained, is the best. Good drainage simply means that your
plants won't be situated in a low spot where water will stand or
where there will be continual dampness. Undrained soil will suffocate the roots of the herb.

It's a good idea to save grass cuttings and sprinkle them
around your herb plants, or to keep weeds away, you may want
to have a load of fine wood chips hauled in and spread around
and between the herb plants. Wood ashes make a good addition
to a garden—but remember our ecology problem and don't burn
wood to pollute the air just to get the ashes! It isn't wise to
fertilize most herbs, for then they will have luxuriant foliage
with very little aromatic oils.

The lists should aid you in selecting herbs that are best suited
to your environment and taste for your outdoor garden.

Herbs that will Grow in Shade

Most herbs grow best in full or partial sun, but the following herbs
will grow successfully in shade.

Perennials: angelica, lemon balm, carpet bugle, sweet cicely, comfrey, costmary, ground ivy, the mints, pennyroyal, French tarragon, wintergreen and sweet woodruff.

Biennials: bugloss, parsley.

Annual: chervil.

Herbs for Ground Cover/Erosion

Perennials: carpet bugle, Roman camomile, ground ivy, thyme, creeping thyme, sweet woodruff and beach wormwood.

Herbs Useful in Landscaping

Before planting your herb garden, check the growing characteristics of each plant. Besides being annual, biennial or perennial, plant sizes and shapes vary, leaf color and texture differs, and height can vary from a few inches (creeping thyme) to about 4′ (southernwood).

Be sure that your tall herbs don't cut off sunlight and air from the smaller ones. Small compact plants look well in front of large many-branched herbs; feathery leaves stand out when backed by large, solid leaves. The following list should help you choose the correct placement of your garden herbs (all are perennials).

Carpet bugle: low, fast-growing plant; leaves variegated or purple; grows 4 to 12″ high.

Creeping thyme: tiny, glossy, green leaves; ground cover, 1″.

Germander: low, dark green, shiny leaves; rosy flowers; hardy edging plant; height 10″.

Ground ivy: like regular ivy except creeping variety, 1″.

Hyssop: shrublike, almost evergreen; pink, blue or white flowers; grows 18″ high.

Lavender: silvery green leaves; purple flowers; grows 12″ high.

Primrose (dwarf Canadian): toothed, blunt, green leaves; pink to pale blue flowers; grows 6″ high.

Roman camomile: lacy, light green leaves; daisylike flowers; height 12″.

Rosemary: silver, spiked leaves; purple blossoms; grows 12″ high.

Rue: bluish green leaves; shrublike plant; yellow flowers; grows 2′ high.

Sage: rough, gray-green leaves; purple flowers; good edging plant; height 2'.

Southernwood: lacy, silver-white leaves; height 4'.

Sweet woodruff: dark green leaves; spires of white flowers; grows 8" high.

Wormwood: silvery white leaves; similar to southernwood; grows 4' high.

Herbs for a Scent Garden

Clove pink: carnation fragrance to foliage and flowers.

Creeping thyme: sharp, pleasant aromatic leaves; aroma rises when walked on.

English lavender: true sweet lavender scent to flowers and leaves.

Garden sage: typical sage taste and fragrance to leaves when crushed.

Geraniums (all kinds): rose, lemon, orange, mint, clove, pineapple, almond.

Heliotrope: very sweet perfume fragrance to flowers when touched.

Lemon balm: sharp, fresh lemon scent and taste to leaves.

Mints (all kinds): apple, lemon, orange, pineapple, spearmint, peppermint.

Pennyroyal: mint-flavored leaves.

Sweet basil: pungent spicy scent to leaves.

Sweet woodruff: delicately fragrant leaves and flowers.

Growing Herbs in Your Garden

Some herbs grow quickly from seed, others are slow and you would be wise to try to find plants from which you can later make cuttings, layerings or root divisions.

To make cuttings from another plant, use a razor blade or very sharp knife to cut a branch or "stem" as close to the base of the parent plant as possible, and cut it on the diagonal, slanting *toward* the parent plant. Usually this location will be where two leaves grow opposite each other. Put the cutting in water or lightly fertilized, moist soil until new roots begin to form; then transplant gently. It's advisable to use a root hormone when transplanting because it prevents shock to the young tender roots, and starts them growing sooner. There are a number of root hormone mixtures on the market; simply follow the directions on the container.

If you are planting young seedlings, use a starter solution. This can be purchased at any nursery, seed store or landscape gardener's shop.

To make a layering, select a branch low on the parent plant, spread it flat on the ground, and cover it firmly with a mound of soil (about a cup) an inch or two from the parent plant; keep moist. Within 2 months, or even the following spring, cut down through the soil nearer the parent plant than the little mound. Gently dig up the newly rooted plant, disturbing the soil around the new roots as little as possible, and transplant.

Root divisions are made by digging up a parent plant and gently shaking it so that the soil falls away from the roots. Examine the root system. You will be able to see that certain groups of stems grow from one portion of the roots, another group from a different portion; pull these apart carefully and replant each division. For example, from a plant of English lavender a year old, you can usually get 4 "new" plants.

Herbs which grow quickly and easily from seed are anise,

basil, borage, burnet, caraway, camomile, chervil, coriander, dill, fennel, lovage, nasturtiums and summer savory. Lemon balm, sweet marjoram, the mints, orégano, the geraniums, parsley, sage, winter savory, rosemary, French tarragon and the thymes will, in almost all locations, thrive better if you will purchase one or more plants and multiply by layering, cutting or root division the following year.

To multiply chives, buy one pot of the plant, take the bulblets out of the pot, shake gently to dislodge the soil, then separate the bulblets and plant each separately. By the end of the first season, you will have new clumps of bulblets to be further divided; or if you let chives seed themselves you will have hundreds of plants! For garlic, buy a few bulbs, peel off the outer skin, separate the individual parts called cloves and plant each separately. As with chives, you'll have a crop at least double in quantity the following season.

The easiest way to get a plentiful growth of annuals is to let them seed themselves. This works well with anise, basil, borage, burnet, camomile, caraway, dill, parsley, sage and the thymes. You'll have to sacrifice harvesting the seeds the first season, but you'll have a much greater harvest the following year.

Depending upon where you live, you may have a little difficulty finding the seeds and plants you want. First try the local seed stores, nurseries and florists and landscape gardeners. Send away for seed catalogs and study them during the winter. Almost every seed house carries some herb seeds and plants. Or send a stamped, self-addressed envelope to the Herb Society of America, Horticultural Hall, Boston, Massachusetts, and request a list of sources for both herb seeds and plants. The U. S. Department of Agriculture publishes pamphlets and booklets about herbs and herb growing. Some of the seed companies that carry herbs are: Asgrow, Burpee, Northrup King, Vaughn, Ferry-Morse and Wayside Gardens. Check garden magazines for advertisements from seed companies throughout the country.

The following illustrated herbs are the most common and most useful culinary herbs that can be grown in your garden. With the exception of the geraniums and rosemary, all the hardy perennials listed will survive in temperature of 20° below zero.

Sweet Basil (*Ocimum basilicum*)

Sweet basil, an annual, is one of the more popular herbs and fortunately an easy one to grow. It propagates from seed and germinates in 4 or 5 days, preferring warm, dry soil and full sun. Basil can grow as high as 2 feet, but my average was 12 to 15 inches. If the first flower buds that appear are pinched off, a full and luscious foliage will develop. Leaf color varies, but the most common is a medium to dark green. Basil can be harvested several times a year if you do not cut the plant back too far. Basil is very vulnerable to frost, so plan your last cutting of the season accordingly. Dry the leaves immediately after harvesting or they will turn black and be useless.

Caraway (*Carum carvi*)

Caraway is a hardy biennial but can be grown as a perennial if every other plant is allowed to go to seed. The seeds are best planted in September so that seeding and flowering will take place the next summer. Germination takes about 14 days; caraway prefers poor soil and full sun. Be sure when planting caraway for the first time to sow the seeds where you want the plant; the roots are quite long and difficult to transplant. Also, because of slow growth, caraway will need care to keep back weeds.

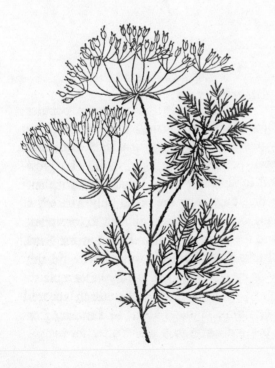

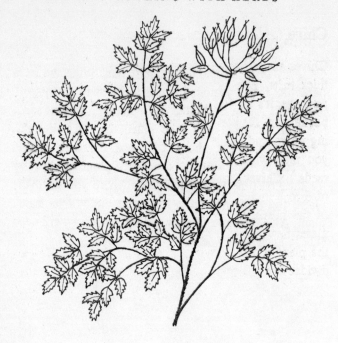

Chervil (*Anthriscus cerefolium*)

Chervil, which resembles parsley, is a low, compact annual (my plants were 6 to 9 inches high) with curly leaves. Chervil prefers sandy, light, moist—but well-drained—soil in shade or partial shade. When planting for the first time, sow the seeds only where you want the plant located, since it is difficult to transplant. Once you find the proper soil, it will self-sow for years, but this will take time. To begin with, you'll probably have to sow in early spring, and perhaps sow again in late spring and then again in fall until the chervil catches on. Germination takes about 14 days, and harvesting can begin about 6 to 8 weeks after sowing.

Chive (*Allium schoenoprasum*)

Chives are self-sowing hardy perennials which grow in thick tufts. You can propagate by seed—just buy one package, it's all you need. Sow in poor soil and full or partial sun. Or you can divide the bulblets of an existing chive and plant. (If you are a first-time grower, you may want to buy the whole plant rather than seeds.) Chives grow very quickly and reach a height of 6 to 8 inches. When harvesting leave 1 or 2 inches of the tubelike leaf above the bulblet. Cutting stimulates new growth, but cutting too far down weakens the plant and may eventually kill it. Chives should be divided every 3 years to avoid choking out.

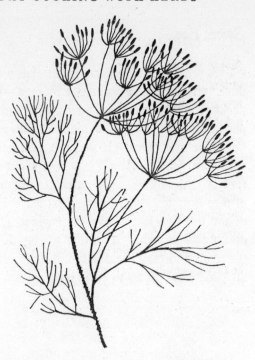

Dill (*Anethum graveolens*)

Dill, an annual, self-sows freely if allowed. Sow in poor soil and full sun, but only where you want the herb. Dill is difficult to transplant because of the long tap-roots; germination takes about 4 or 5 days. Dill adds a decorative touch to any outdoor garden with its feathery leaves, flower umbels which house the seeds, and the 3-foot-high growth. You can snip the leaves and use them fresh while in season or freeze them for later use. Harvest the seeds when they just turn brown. Snip and tie branches, and place in a paper bag to dry. Then, shake the bag to dislodge the seeds; remove, and store in an airtight container until you're ready to use.

Sweet Fennel (*Foeniculum vulgare*)

Sweet fennel, a hardy perennial, is one of the more versatile culinary herbs; the seeds, leaves and stalks are all edible. All have been used for centuries both as a food and medicine—from reducing pills (seeds), to snacks (stalks), to food-flavor-enhancer (foliage), to cure bad eyesight (a mixture)! Fennel prefers sweet soil, plenty of moisture, and full sun; it grows to a height of 2 to 4 feet. Propagation is by seed, and germination takes about 10 days. The feathery bright-green leaves, the umbels of tiny yellow flowers, and the delicate aniselike scent add a waft of graceful beauty to any herb garden.

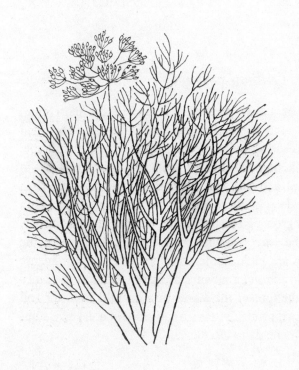

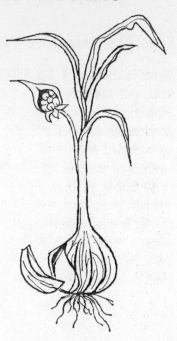

Garlic (*Allium sativum*)

Garlic, a hardy perennial, is one of the most commonly used herbs. Propagation is best accomplished by purchasing bulbs, peeling off the outer membrane, and planting the divided sections—called cloves—in rich soil and full sun. Plant the cloves no more than 1 inch deep in the soil. Each clove will produce a bulb in one growing season. Garlic can reach a height of 2 feet; the leaves are flat and about 1 inch wide; the flowers are pink. Some cooks snip the leaves and use them in the same manner as chives. Harvest the bulbs when the tops of the leaves turn dry; lift from the soil and dry thoroughly. Be sure to store in a dry place until you're ready to use them.

Sweet Marjoram (*Majorana hortensis*)

Sweet marjoram, a perennial, is quite susceptible to frost, and therefore is grown as an annual in the north. Propagation is most easily accomplished by using root divisions or cuttings, and planting them in warm, dry, well-drained soil in full sun. Marjoram is one of the beauties of the herb garden. It grows to a height of 8 to 12 inches; the stems are purplish, the leaves a soft-textured green-gray with a soft downlike covering, the flowers a cream color. Marjoram is also a useful plant —oil to scent soap is made from the top of the plant, the leaves are used for flavoring food, and the whole plant is used medicinally for nervous headaches.

Mint (*Mentha*)

There are many different varieties of mints and all are hardy perennials. Favorites among the herb growers are spearmint, peppermint and three mints with fruity overtones—apple mint, pineapple mint and orange mint. They enjoy moist, rich soil in partial shade. Germination is slow; so to begin growing, buy a full-grown plant and divide the roots. Spearmint has erect reddish stems, glossy narrow leaves and pale lavender flowers. Peppermint has dark green stems and leaves, and profuse purple flowers. Apple mint is a low-growing plant with smooth, bright-green leaves variegated with pale yellow, and lilac flower spikes. Pineapple mint has woolly green leaves variegated in pale yellow and white, and yellow flowers. Orange mint has reddish stems, violet-edged green leaves, and purple blossoms.

Orégano (*Origanum vulgare*)

Orégano, also called "wild marjoram," is a hardy perennial that grows into a leafy bush about 2 feet high. It has tiny purple-rose-colored flowers and deep green leaves; but of course, if you allow the flowers to bloom, less foliage will develop and your snippings will not be as tasty. Germination is slow; so it's best to purchase a full-grown plant and divide the roots. Orégano prefers good soil, well-drained, and full sun. The best time to harvest orégano is when the tiny flower buds begin to open (2 or 3 times a year). Although you can cut orégano back drastically, be sure to leave at least a third of the stem and leaves on the plant so it can recover.

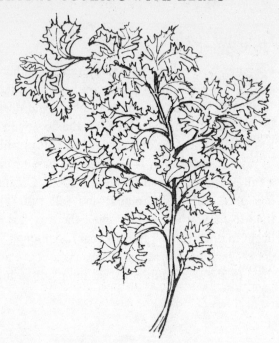

Parsley (*Petroselinum crispum*)

Parsley is probably the most widely known and used culinary herb. It is a biennial, but if allowed to self-sow in a bed, can be grown as a perennial. Some gardeners consider parsley difficult to grow because of the long germination period—3 to 6 weeks. Germination can be hastened by soaking the seeds in warm water for 24 hours before sowing. Sow in medium-rich soil (add plenty of compost) and partial sun. Water plentifully, but not so much as to suffocate the roots with undrained water or constant dampness. Parsley makes an attractive border or edging with its 4- to 6-inch-high crisp, curly, bright-green leaves. If you want to harvest your parsley for winter use, you can dry or freeze the leaves. When drying, do not allow the parsley to turn brown, for then it is flavorless.

Rosemary (*Rosmarinus officinalis*)

Rosemary, a tender perennial, is perhaps the most lovely and fragrant of the herbs. The leaves are silvery-gray and very narrow, almost fernlike; the flowers range in color from pale purple to pale blue. Rosemary is best grown from root divisions or cuttings because of the long germination period; seeds take about 6 months. Place the plants in dry, light soil that is alkaline in sun or partial shade. Rosemary is winter-killed in northern states, so it should be brought in and potted during the very cold months. Usually rosemary will grow to about 1 foot high, but if conditions are right and the plant is taken care of, it will reach a height of 4 or 5 feet.

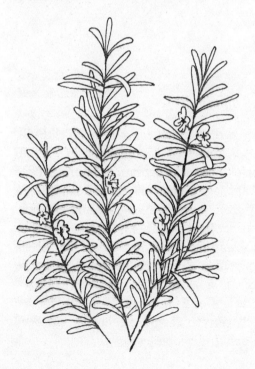

Sage (*Salvia officinalis*)

Sage is a hardy perennial that can survive all climates. It can be grown from seed—germination in 7 to 10 days—but you also can take cuttings or layerings from an existing plant. Sage prefers full sun and sandy, light soil. The gray-green leaves are long, slender and pebbly; the flowers are light purple. You can harvest 2 or 3 times a year; snip the leaves just before the flowers open, dry and store in airtight containers. Sage can be used attractively as a hedge in your outdoor garden—it grows to a height of 2 to 4 feet. However, for the best-tasting foliage, you should continually cut back the plant to promote thick, bushy growth.

Savory, Summer (*Satureja hortensis*) or Winter (*Satureja montana*)

Summer savory is a self-sowing annual which is most easily propagated by seed; germination takes from 10 to 14 days. It is a slender plant, from 16 to 18 inches high, with small, narrow leaves and tubular purple flowers. You can take snippings all summer, but in fall, pull up the whole plant and dry for winter use. Winter savory, a hardy perennial that grows from 12 to 15 inches, is best propagated by root division. The leaves are gray-green and needlelike; the flowers are white, pink or purple. Winter savory will stay green all season if you protect it in cold climates by placing a basket over it or spreading mulch around its roots. Harvest just before flowering, dry and store. Both savories like poor soil, good drainage and full sun.

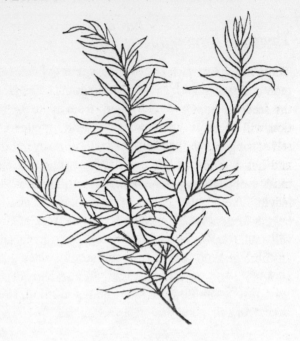

Tarragon (*Artemisia dracunculus*)

French tarragon is one of the few herbs that is not known to produce seeds, so propagation can be accomplished only by taking root divisions or cuttings from an existing plant. Be sure to get the French variety and not the Russian tarragon, as the latter is inedible. French tarragon is a hardy perennial whose roots should be divided every 3 years because they have a tendency to strangle the plant after a length of time. Tarragon needs well-drained, moderately rich soil in partial shade. The leaves are long, narrow and shiny green; the flowers, white and sterile.

Thyme (*Thymus vulgaris*)

There are many varieties of thyme, but the most common culinary variety is English or garden thyme. Sow the seeds in poor soil and a sunny location; germination will occur in about 10 days. English thyme is a self-sowing perennial that grows to a 12-inch height and has a tendency to spread. The herb gives an almost evergreen appearance with its oblong, tapering leaves. The leaves are a dark green on top and gray on the bottom; the flowers are pale lavender. Thyme will make an excellent addition to a rock garden, or any herb garden.

Growing Less Common Culinary Herbs

ANISE (*Pimpinella anisum*): *Propagation* by seed but does not transplant well. An *annual*, it seeds itself if flower heads are allowed to mature and dry. Likes *poor soil, well-drained. Appearance:* Grows to a height of about 2 feet, leaves are broad and finely notched with a lacy look. The flower umbel or seed head is similar to dill. Grows in *sun* or *partial shade.*

BALM, LEMON (*Melissa officinalis*): *Propagation* is fastest if a single plant is purchased and cuttings taken or root division made the following season. Seeds take several months to germinate. Very hardy *perennial.* Likes *slightly sandy, well-drained soil. Appearance:* Low growing, compact little plant, leaves bright green, pebbly and rounded.

BORAGE (*Borago officinalis*): *Propagation* by seed, germinates easily, self-sows freely. *Annual,* grows 2 or 3 feet tall, likes *poor soil, sun. Appearance:* Large, rough-textured light green leaves, blue flower clusters.

BURNET (*Sanguisorba officinalis*): *Propagation* by seed, self-sows freely and can be propagated further by root division in spring. Hardy *perennial.* Likes *poor soil, full sun. Appearance:* Attractive low bushy plant with light green, sharply notched small leaves, pink flower stalks.

CAMOMILE, ROMAN (*Anthemis nobilis*): *Propagation* by seed, quick and easy germination. Hardy *perennial,* prefers *poor soil, sun or shade.* Makes an excellent ground cover, can be mowed or walked on. *Appearance:* Light, very fine lacy green leaves, small daisylike flowers; grows about 1 inch tall.

LOVAGE (*Levisticum officinale*): *Propagation* by seed or by root division. Hardy *perennial.* Grows well in *any soil, sun or partial shade. Appearance:* Attractive, somewhat tropical foliage with small insignificant white flowerets.

NASTURTIUM (*Tropaeolum majus*): *Propagation* by seed in 7 or 8 days. Tender *annual*. Prefers *light, sandy soil* in *full sun*. *Appearance:* Round, low plants about 8 inches high with round, veined leaves and flowers ranging from pale yellow to orange, red and russet.

ROSE GERANIUM (*Pelargonium graveolens*): *Propagation* by cuttings; buy 1 plant and make cuttings for full-grown plants the following season. Prefers *rich soil* in *sun or partial shade*. The geraniums are *tender perennials* and should be brought inside in cold climates; they make most attractive house plants. There are many other varieties of scented geraniums: apple, mint, clove, walnut, filbert, lemon, orange, pineapple, lime, cinnamon, nutmeg, almond and apricot. *Appearance:* All have leaves which are large and deeply notched; some varieties have furry leaves, other are smooth and shiny. Flowers are small but very fragrant. Most varieties 8 to 12 inches tall.

Have you missed bay leaves or some of your other herb favorites in this gardener's list? Here are reasons why you're not likely to be growing the following herbs in American culinary herb gardens.

ANGELICA, while not difficult to grow, has no culinary use except as candied stalks and in some commercial candies. The leaves may be blanched and eaten like celery, but lovage is better. The plant is very tall and awkward. Candied angelica can be purchased in most gourmet food stores.

BAY LEAF is the leaf of mountain laurel, grown in Greece, Spain and Portugal, and parts of Asia. Our native mountain laurel does not have the true taste, and the European variety doesn't grow well in our climate.

CAPERS are the flower buds of a European shrub which does not grow in the United States. The mature but not dry seeds of nasturtiums make an excellent substitute for capers if pickled.

CARDAMOM grows in India and Mexico but will not thrive in the United States.

CORIANDER, although not difficult to grow, is unsuitable for the garden because of the extremely foul smell of the leaves. The seeds are the only usable part of the plant, and it's easier to buy ground coriander at the market than to go through the complicated process of harvesting the seeds and grinding them yourself.

CUMIN will not grow in the United States; it is cultivated for commercial use in Africa, Europe and Mexico.

HORSERADISH is easy to grow but the process of grinding or grating the roots is such a "tearful" task, it's easier to buy the fresh ground horseradish at the market.

LEEKS are grown extensively in England and Wales, as well as in southern Europe. They must be grown in trenches covered with straw to make them tender and bleach the tops; they are kept very wet and must be hand cultivated.

MUSTARD is easy to grow but it's so bothersome to watch for the seed to reach the exact state of ripeness necessary for the full flavor. Mustard is grown commercially for seed in California.

PAPRIKA is the sweet red pepper dried and powdered; it is grown commercially throughout Europe. The drying and pulverizing process is slow and tedious.

POPPY SEED can be grown in the United States, but again, the plants require constant watching to harvest the seeds, for when they are ripe the seed pods "explode" and it's extremely difficult to gather the tiny seeds.

SAFFRON is grown in Europe and Asia. The yellow powder comes from the dried stigmas of a species of crocus. It takes 75,000 blossoms to produce 1 pound of saffron. The blossoms must be hand-picked.

SESAME is grown in India, China and southern Asia. It's difficult to grow sesame in the United States, and since the seeds are the only part of the plant used, it's more practical to buy them.

SHALLOTS are grown commercially in England, France and Switzerland. They must be grown in greenhouses in the United States.

SORREL or "sour grass" grows wild throughout the United States but is difficult to "tame" or cultivate. The shield-shaped pale green leaves are ready to eat at the same time as dandelion greens; they're delicious in salads.

The Best Way to Dry Your Own Herbs

If you have an herb garden and want to harvest herbs to dry for winter use, here is the best way to do it. Cut a piece of window screening ½ inch smaller all around than the rack in your oven.

Cut the herbs and wash them thoroughly, leaving the leaves on the stems. Let them dry on a bath towel or paper towels until the residual moisture has evaporated.

Lay the herbs on the screening, place on the oven rack and turn the oven to the *lowest possible heat,* leaving the oven door open.

The herbs will dry in 2 to 4 hours, depending upon how large the leaves are and the humidity of the room. Don't place herbs more than an inch deep on the screening. When you feel, by touching them, that the leaves are crisp and dry, strip the leaves from the stems and crumble them, fine or coarse as you prefer. Place in a clean jar and leave the lid off. If, within 24 hours, there appears to be moisture on the sides of the jar, they must be dried longer. Place foil, paper towels, or cheesecloth on the screening, sprinkle the crumbled herbs on this and return them to the oven for further drying. When no sign of moisture appears in the jar after this drying, cap tightly and store in a cool, dark place.

This is a more satisfactory way to dry herbs than hanging them in bunches in an attic or other warm place. Quick drying in the low-heat oven preserves color and aroma.

How to Grow Herbs Indoors and Under Artificial Light

Growing herbs indoors gives you the opportunity to create the atmosphere of "something green" year round. The variety of textures and rich green hues add interest to any room and the benefits of having fresh herbs at your fingertips is such a culinary treat. In some instances, the fragrance of the foliage alone would make the growing worthwhile.

The best way to start your indoor garden is either to purchase established herb plants or bring them in from your outdoor garden. Propagation of indoor as well as outdoor herbs can be accomplished from cuttings, root divisions or seeds. At the end of this chapter, I have included the most common culinary varieties found in indoor gardens. All recommended herbs will thrive indoors, given the same growing medium and treatment.

The growing medium may be organic (soil) or a sterilized commercially packaged growing medium such as Jiffy Mix, Redi-Earth, Cornell Mix or Black Magic. These packaged mixes may have too fine a texture, but you can mix in equal amounts of builder's sand and either peat moss or chopped sphagnum moss. Because these mixtures are usually very dry, they need special treatment before you pot your herbs. Place in a bucket or tub, mix well with very hot water. Allow the mixture to absorb the water until cool, then wring out the excess. Now it's ready to be used for potting.

Organic growing medium has the advantage of innate richness and texture. You can use either natural leaf mold or screened compost. However, the big disadvantage of organic soil is that it can contain weed seeds and disease elements in the form of fungi, bacteria or insects.

Leaf mold or compost contains valuable nutrients in the form of decayed organic matter. But even these leach out or are used up by the plant. The sterilized mediums may have some nutrients, but will need a fertilizer boost. These elements are to the plants as vitamins are to humans. Since herbs are valued for their foliage, a fertilizer with a high proportion of nitrogen to phosphorous and potassium, such as 10-5-5, may be used.

How often should you fertilize container-grown herbs? The longer the period of light, the more the plant will be using nurtrients and growing. You may apply chemical fertilizers (mixed with water according to package directions) every 2 weeks at the height of the growing season. During the dull winter days, apply on an average of every 6 weeks. Vary the application time as the growing season approaches and recedes. Do not make a soluble solution stronger than is indicated on the package. It is possible to "burn" the plant tissues and kill the plant with an overdose of chemicals. If you use a slow-acting organic fertilizer, such as dehydrated cow manure, you need apply only 2 to 4 times a year.

Of the two major kinds of containers for growing plants—clay and plastic—clay is porous and allows for good drainage and air circulation. But because of the porosity, the growing medium dries out faster. Herbs in plastic pots can survive a weekend without being watered, but the growing medium can become sodden due to overwatering and lack of air circulation.

All containers for herbs should allow for adequate drainage (particularly plastic) by having both a drainage hole in the bottom and drainage material over the hole. (If you prefer plastic, look for the containers that have drainage *slits* rather than just holes.) Drainage material can consist of overlapping pieces of broken clay pot or several layers of pebbles or perlite and should be placed directly over the drainage holes or slits. This material not only allows for proper drainage, but stops growing medium from washing out or blocking the drainage holes of the container.

Herbs are found naturally within the temperate zone. This means that they grow best in moderate temperatures ranging from a low of 60° at night to a high of 80° during the day. With photosynthesis occurring during the day, the plant gives off energy during the night (dark period) and this expansion, or actual growing, occurs optimally with a 10° drop in temperature nightly. However, herbs should not be placed where they will be in a draft or the leaves will wilt, since evaporation of water from the leaves occurs faster than the plant can supply water from the root area. At the same time, some air circulation assures the replenishment of carbon dioxide and tends to prevent fungi and bacteria from developing on the plant.

How much must you water herbs indoors? Generally, 2 or 3 times a week. As you know, the higher the temperature, the faster the growing medium will dry out. Don't wait for the plants to wilt (hang limp, due to lack of water which holds the plant firm). Feel the top surface of the growing medium between your fingers. When it becomes dry enough to pulverize easily, it's time to water your herbs.

When potting, be sure to allow for ½-inch space from the top of the container to the top of your growing medium. Fill this space with water gently, but all in one step to insure that the plant is watered thoroughly. Always water from the top, and never allow the container to sit continuously in water, because plant roots will rot. If the container is sitting in water after an hour, pour or suction off all the excess. Herbs will need to be watered *more often* if you see lots of new young leaves. Hanging herbs generally will need to be watered more often than those planted in conventional clay pots, and those in the clay pots will need to be watered more often than those in plastic.

Another form of water as important to herbs as it is to humans is humidity which is ideal for both at 50 per cent. A lot of rooms in the winter have only 20 per cent humidity. Try a misting atomizer to cover the foliage with a fine spray. Or, set up a tray of pebbles or perlite for the containers to sit upon. The pebble layer will hold the container above the water which runs off. Be sure that the water level in the pebble tray never reaches the containers. (A pebble tray, if made of metal, should be treated with a rust inhibitor or should be made of rustproof galvanized iron.) The run-off water will evaporate, providing higher humidity around the herbs. Another arrangement is to fit wire screening over a tray; the containers will sit on the screening and the tray will hold the run-off for evaporation.

Most herbs have good light in their natural habitat. Generally, then, the best place in the home to locate growing herbs is in a west or south window. But even in the sunniest windows, herbs actually receive only 40 per cent of the light they need, due to the vertical angle of the window panes. Window panes also get dirty! And perhaps trees or buildings obstruct the light. If light is inadequate, plants will lean toward the panes to get all the light they can. This won't happen if you use artifical lighting.

Sunshine supplies the full spectrum of color waves, but plants use primarily blue and red color for their growth. Blue (cool) light helps the plant "breathe" and grow bushy, while red (warm) light helps leaf growth. It is possible to use a combination of standard fluorescent bulbs, but various companies have developed fluorescent bulbs specifically for indoor gardens. These bulbs combine precisely the blue and red color waves needed for growing plants. For each square foot of indoor plant material you need 10 to 20 watts of plant fluorescent bulbs, or 20 to 40 watts of combined standard daylight (blue) and warm (red) fluorescent bulbs. It is not necessary to combine incandescent lighting in your setup when growing herbs because you want lush foliage and not flowers.

Plant fluorescents come in various sizes and shapes. You can use the standard fixture setups which hold 1 to 4 bulbs. Try to set up your indoor herb garden using long bulbs. If working with limited space, such as a cabinet or bookcase, you can double up with 2 shorter bulbs in the small space.

Every fluorescent light setup should have a reflector, not only to deflect the light, but also to diffuse the light toward the plants. The inside of the reflector, if not coated with titanium oxide, should be painted flat white. When working in a bookcase, for instance, and there is no space for a reflector, paint the inside of the bookcase flat white. If you wish to hide the source of light, you may create the effect of recessed lighting by simply adding a valance of wood or fabric, or design a covering suitable to your decorating theme.

Burn the lights 14 to 16 hours a day to simulate the period of outdoor photosynthesis. There is a timing device on the market which will automatically switch the lights on and off. Even if you don't start out with an automatic timing device, you may want to incorporate one at a future date. In this case, be sure *not* to get the short-circuit, push-button-type starter, for you cannot adapt this type to automatic lighting later.

Fluorescent lights have a life expectancy of 10,000 to 20,000 hours (or 2 to 4 years), but after about 2 years the lights are no longer giving maximum light for plant growth. You won't notice the difference, but the plants will.

Herbs at different stages of their lives need different intensities of light. Fluorescent bulbs should be positioned no farther than 12 to 14 inches away from mature plants. But for germinating seeds, bulbs should almost touch the containers; 2-inch seedlings should be 6 inches below the bulbs. To increase the light intensity: (1) have a setup which is adjustable, or raise the containers; (2) place the containers near the middle of the lighted area; (3) add more bulbs or (4) compensate by lengthening exposure time.

The following companies manufacture plant fluorescent bulbs:

Duro-Test Corporation
2321 Kennedy Boulevard
North Bergen, New Jersey 07047

"Vitalite"
(soft white with a
gentle misty cast)

Sylvania Indoor Lighting
1704 Barnes Street
Reidsville, North Carolina 27320

"Gro-Lux"
(lavender with a
cold blue cast)

Westinghouse Electric Corporation
1 Westinghouse Plaza
Bloomfield, New Jersey 07003

"Plant-Gro"
(yellow with a slightly
green cast)

A large plant, used as a decorator item to soften architectural lines, can stand alone dramatically. But most herb plants are small and should be grouped for effective appearance. A pebble tray cut to fit the space exactly will give a finished appearance to a group of potted herbs. (Place a sheet of plastic between the tray and your painted surface.) Try to have all containers of the same material and of neutral coloring so as not to detract from the growing plants. If the area is a fairly large flat surface, create different levels by raising some pots of herbs on columns or pedestals of glass, clear plastic, or risers that enhance the beauty of your plants. Or use chains or hooks to hang some herbs above the others. Remember that a hanging herb will need to be watered more often because of its exposure to more air circulation.

Whether you bring herbs in from your outdoor garden or purchase them, use only the healthiest of plants. Sometimes the purchase price of healthy plants is higher initially, but well worth it in resistance to pests and diseases.

For an indoor garden, choose herbs that you especially like in your cooking. Start with a few simple varieties and then add to your collection. Basil, thyme, savory and orégano could be the first few plants; then, progress to chives, sage and tarragon. Others which can be well adapted to growing indoors are marjoram, burnet, lemon balm, parsley, mint and rosemary. You may want to add scented geraniums just for their wonderful fragrance. If you wish to add some nonculinary herbs to your display for color, a good choice could be either dwarf impatiens, African violets or geraniums. (Position flowering geraniums where they will receive maximum light intensity.) Or for fresh, gay color, tuck in pots of inexpensive seasonal flowering plants, such as paper-white narcissus, blue hyacinths, chrysanthemums or poinsettias.

When you live with herbs indoors, enjoy them and remember their needs. Give them the cultural care they will need to look their best; remove dying leaves and snip the tips of the top and side branches frequently. Since you are interested in the tasty leaves, do not allow the flower buds to develop; they will drain the plant of energy needed to produce lush foliage. To prevent pests, it is a good practice to wash the plants regularly with plain water every 2 to 4 weeks. When possible, apply a forceful showering of cold water to the underside of the leaves.

Your herbs will respond to your devotion by producing luxuriant plants from which you will reap with pride the delicious foliage. You will add flavor-sparkle to every day. Be imaginative. For instance, start the day off by serving scrambled eggs with chives, add dill to the creamed shrimp, toss basil into that salad or stir mint into your tea. You will feel much satisfaction in creating dishes that contain herbs you've grown.

Herbs Make Glamorous Gifts

There are a dozen different ways you can package and present herbs to your friends. And what charming (and inexpensive) gifts they make at Christmastime, for birthday or anniversary remembrances, or just to say, "I'm thinking of you."

Follow the recipes in this book to make herb jellies, Herb Mustard, Herb French Dressing, herb wine vinegars and herb blends; then package them for your friends. Or, follow the directions given here and send someone a fragrant Herb Sachet or Herb Potpourri.

Packaging Your Herb Gift

If you save bottles and jars from supermarket purchases, you'll literally have free packaging for your gifts. Or you can buy small jars and bottles in quantity—see your pharmacist or consult the Yellow Pages. Be sure that all the bottles and jars you use have good tight screw tops.

Jellies are ideally packed in small jars like baby food jars or small-size olive or pickle jars, 2 to 4 ounces. Pour Herb French Dressing into 8-ounce bottles and pack Herb Mustard in 8-ounce jars; box them together for a truly unique gift—there's nothing like them on the market. Collect 8-ounce and 3-ounce bottles for the herb wine vinegars.

To prepare jars for filling, wash them thoroughly and sterilize both jars and lids by placing them in boiling water for about 20 minutes. Stand jars upside down on paper towels to drain and dry; then fill and cap as directed below.

Painting the jar lids, decorating the bottles or designing your own label will add that precious personal touch to your gifts. The labels are easy: Use pressure-sensitive paper and fine felt pens in bright colors. The paper comes in squares, strips, ovals and plain sheets so you can find or cut a shape and size appropriate to your jars. Pack the jars in a fluff of colored tissue paper or a nest of Easter grass and place them in a small gift box or wicker basket; trim with ribbon if you wish.

Herb Jellies

Make all 7 jelly recipes (see Index) so you'll be able to pack each gift box with 2 or more flavors. Fill the jars to within ½ inch of the top and cover with a thin layer of hot paraffin. An attractive combination for Christmas would be green Apple Mint Jelly and Spiced Ruby Cranberry Jelly.

Herb Mustard and Herb French Dressing

Expect to be asked for refills if you present either of these two gourmet treats (see Index). They were my 2 best sellers when I marketed Scotch Ridge products. Now they are yours for the making. Fill sterilized mustard jars to the brim and seal with tight screw tops. Sterilize bottles for the dressing, fill to the top and cap tightly. Use your artistry (or copy a design you like) to make distinctive labels. Or you may want to add "From the kitchen of — (your name)."

Herb Blends

Bottle your homemade blends of Herb Salt, Salad Herbs, Savory Blend, Fines Herbes and Bouquet Garni (see Index) in 1-ounce bottles of clear plastic. The bottles with snap-lock tops which pharmacists use are ideal—ask your druggist to sell you the quantity you want. They cost only a few cents each. Pack 2, 3, 4 or more in small gift boxes decorated for the occasion.

Herb Wine Vinegars

Follow the recipes in this book (see Index) for making your own herb-flavored wine vinegars, and set the jugs aside to age as directed. When the vinegars have aged, you can bottle them in 3- or 8-ounce bottles, adding a sprig of the appropriate herb to each bottle—dill, tarragon, mint or basil. It's best to strain the chives, garlic and burnet vinegars. Two of the large-size bottles make an elegant gift, or you might box a variety pack of 3 or 4 of the 3-ounce bottles.

Herb Sachets

If you have any roses growing in your garden, or if you receive a gift of roses, save the petals. Sprinkle them in a large, shallow bowl and allow to dry naturally, in a dry, dark place. The time it takes for them to dry depends upon the quantity; the petals from a dozen roses will take about 3 weeks to dry. Save the flower stalks from English lavender and the blossoms from any other fragrant herbs you may have, such as carnations, lavender, anise, the geraniums, the mints, rosemary and fennel. Simply add these to the rose petals and allow them to dry all together. Every few days, stir them lightly with your fingers so that the blooms on the bottom of the bowl will be aerated and will dry more evenly. I use a large salad bowl 15 inches in diameter and 5 inches deep, and from the first blooms of spring until the frost, I keep this bowl filled with petals and blossoms. As one bowlful dries, I transfer the contents to a wide-mouth gallon jar with a tight lid and store in a dark place. By the end of summer the gallon jar is usually full.

When you have the quantity of petals and blossoms you want, *for each cup* of blooms, add a pinch of cinnamon, 2 or 3 whole cloves, and ½ teaspoon of orrisroot—you can buy this at most good pharmacies. A large dishpan is good for mixing.

During the summer while you are waiting for the blooms to dry, you could make the sachet bags. Buy satin ribbon 2 inches wide in pastel colors—pink, lavender, yellow, light blue, pale green (use white satin ribbon for brides). Cut ribbon in 4-inch lengths. You will get 9 sachet bags from 1 yard of ribbon. Reverse the ribbon and fold in half to make 2-inch squares. Stitch the 2 sides together, reverse again, satin side out, and stuff with the flower petal mixture. Close opening by hand with tiny stitches, and finish off with a little bow of matching or contrasting baby ribbon in one corner. Three to 6 sachets packed in a flat gift box make delightful gifts. The fragrance lasts at least 2 years. If you have more of the flower-sachet mixture than you need for a season, screw the top of the jar tightly and store in a dark, dry place—the sachet mixture itself will last for 2 years.

Herb Potpourris

Using the same blend of flower petals and spices you mixed for sachets, fill a rose jar or any hand-painted jar of your own. The jar should have a lid that can be removed easily to allow the delightful blend of fragrances to perfume the room.

INDEX

Q

SELECTED INDEX OF HERB USAGE

The locations of primary description of the herb and its ordinary preparation are printed in **boldface type.**

The common useful culinary herbs that are easily grown in the Northern Hemisphere can be found on pages 182–97. The drawings illustrate their ordinary appearance.

Less common or horticulturally difficult herbs that grow in Africa, Asia, India, Europe, and Mexico are listed on pages 198–201.

HERB	APPETIZERS	SOUPS/STEWS	SALADS	BEVERAGES	EGGS/CHEESE
ANISE	Sweet cream cheese	Seeds in some stews	Fruit salads	Teas, Fruit drinks	
BASIL	Dips, Canapés	All kinds	Green salads, Tomato aspic	Tomato juice	Omelets, Rarebits
BORAGE	Mild dips	All kinds	Green salads, Coleslaw	Iced drinks	
BURNET	Dips, Canapés	Cream soups	Green salads, Potato salad	Iced drinks	
CARAWAY	Spreads, Canapés	Potato soup, Goulash	Coleslaw, Potato salad		Cream cheese, Cottage cheese
CHIVES	All kinds	All kinds	All kinds		Omelets, Cheese dishes, Deviled eggs
DILL	All kinds	Potato, All kinds as garnish	Green salads, Coleslaw, Potato salad	Tomato juice	Cheese spreads, Omelets
MARJORAM	Cream cheese	All kinds	Green salads, Chicken salad	Vegetable cocktails	Omelets, Scrambled eggs
MINTS		Green pea, Split pea	Fruit salads	Teas, Iced drinks	
OREGANO	Spreads, Canapés	Onion soup, All stews	Seafood, Aspics		Omelets, Spicy cheese
PARSLEY	All kinds	All kinds	All kinds	Vegetable cocktails	Omelets, Cheeses
ROSEMARY	Cheese dips	All kinds	Chicken, Seafood	Vegetable juices	Omelets, Sharp cheese
SAGE	Cheese dips	Cream soups, Chowders			Sharp cheese, Cottage cheese
SAVORY	Cheese dips	Bean soup, Chowders	Aspics, Green salads	Vegetable cocktails	Deviled eggs, Omelets
TARRAGON	All kinds	Chicken, Mushroom	All kinds	Vegetable cocktails	Omelets, Cream cheese
THYME	Shrimp dip	Vegetable, All stews	Tomato aspic	Lemon tea	Cottage cheese, Cream cheese